ROBERT ADAM

ARCHITECTURAL

The Journal of the Architectural Heritage Society of Scotland

HERITAGE IV

ROBERT ADAM

Architectural Heritage Society of Scotland
1993
Distributed by Edinburgh University Press

The Architectural Heritage Society of Scotland
Glasite Meeting House
33 Barony Street
Edinburgh EH6 6WX
Tel: (031) 557 0019

Manuscripts for submission to *Architectural Heritage* should be sent to John Lowrey, c/o the Architectural Heritage Society of Scotland, as above.

Architectural Heritage IV is the twentieth issue of the *Journal of the Architectural Heritage Society of Scotland* (formerly the *Scottish Georgian Society*). Backnumbers (1,7-11,13,15) are available from the Society. *Architectural Heritage I: William Adam* (1990), *Architectural Heritage II: Scottish Architects Abroad* (1991) and *Architectural Heriatge III: The Age of Adam* (1992) are available directly from Edinburgh University Press.

Membership of the Society entitles members to receive both *Architectural Heritage* and the regular *Newsletters* free of charge. The Society exists to promote the protection and study of Scotland's historic architecture. Details of membership can be obtained from the Society's headquarters.

Transferred to digital print 2004

Printed and bound in Great Britain by
Marston Book Services Limited, Oxford

ISBN 0 7486 0462 6

CONTENTS

FOREWORD

I am delighted than Historic Scotland is able to sponsor this issue of the *Journal of the Architectural Heritage Society of Scotland* on Robert Adam and that Ranald MacInnes, one of our Principal Inspectors of Historic Buildings is a major contributor.

If there is one Scottish architect whose name is known throughout Great Britain and beyond it is Robert Adam, although Charles Rennie Mackintosh, the subject of an earlier *Journal*, cannot now be far behind. The name of Adam is bandied around with about as much imprecision as estate agents reserve for 'Georgian'. Indeed, it has virtually entered the English language alongside such trade names as Hoover and Thermos. 'Adam-style' fireplaces, cornices, door furniture and other derivatives are now stocked in D-I-Y stores alongside the patio doors and double glazing. If the sincerest form of flattery is imitation, then Robert Adam clearly has his place in the Pantheon of household gods.

But there is a world of difference between being 'known' and being understood and properly appreciated. There are many furth of Scotland who are ignorant of Robert Adam's work north of the border. A guest from southern England in a well-known Scottish house was recently heard to express surprise that Robert Adam had been active so far north! So much for Charlotte Square, Gosford House, Dumfries House .... but before we indulge in an easy Scottish smugness about this solecism we should consider how much we know about Robert Adam. 'I kent his faither' is the traditional Caledonian put-down for those who have made good, but how many Scots know about William Adam and his works and the context and training he provided for his sons?
The essays in the *Journal* are of value because they cause us to question our assumption that we 'know' Robert Adam simply because we have visited and enjoyed some of the fruits of his genius. We will all have our favourites - the libraries at Mellerstain and Kenwood, the functionality of Register House, the monumental qualities of Culzean and Dalquharran and the charm of the garden folly at Auchincruive. Robert Adam is an old friend but it is all too easy to take old friends for granted. Friendships are deepened by critical re-appraisal and a sympathetic seeking for greater understanding. New knowledge needs to be gathered and analysed. We should be grateful to Ian Gow and John Lowrey for commissioning the contributions to this *Journal* and editing it.

No-one could say that Robert Adam is a prophet without honour in his own country. On the other hand his message should shine more brightly in the light of these stimulating and thought-provoking essays.

GRAEME MUNRO
Director and Chief Executive
Historic Scotland

EDITORIAL

This volume of the *Journal of the Architectural Heritage Society of Scotland* is based on proceedings of the Society's 1992 conference, *Robert Adam: The Scottish Legacy,* which was the culmination of a series of events marking the bicentenary of the architect's death. The articles in this volume are based on the papers delivered at this conference (the authors are indicated in the text) with some extra, related material added by authors who were working in the same area of research. In addition, the *Journal* is proud to continue its association with the Colin McWilliam Memorial Lecture, with the publication of the fourth in this series.

As the conference title suggests, the emphasis in this issue is firmly on the Scottish context of Robert Adam's work; there are articles on personal and family matters as well as his architecture. Indeed, one thing to emerge from the essays in this volume is that there is a close connection between these two areas. The issue here is not so much Adam's legacy to Scotland, although his influence in Scotland and beyond is discussed, and, it might be argued, that the Scottish works constitute his legacy to us all: namely the buildings themselves. Of far greater importance however, is the issue of the rich legacy of Scottish architecture to which Adam was heir, and its impact on his work. Several articles are specifically concerned with this issue and the authors demonstrate how Adam drew from a wide range of Scottish architecture, especially the Court Style of the late sixteenth and seventeenth century; the traditions of Scottish castellated architecture, and, not least, the architecture of William Adam, his own father. As well as these specific influences, it also becomes clear that Robert Adam shared the general Scots concern with monumentality in architecture, a concern he shared with many of those in the vanguard of European Neo-classicism.

Adam's most quoted statement about Scotland is that it was a 'narrow country' (a statement dealt with by both Ranald MacInnes and Margaret Sanderson in their articles). What the essays in this volume show is that Scotland may have been narrow in terms of opportunity, but certainly not in terms of inspiration.

Apart from Robert Adam, the most frequently mentioned individual in this volume is Ian Gow of the NMRS. The Society, the editor and a number of the authors are in his debt since he was responsible for the organisation of the excellent conference on which the *Journal* is based and has played a major part in the preparation of a number of the items for publication.

The Society is grateful to Historic Scotland who have provided a very generous grant towards the costs of this publication and to the Department of Architecture, University of Edinburgh, for technical assistance

Editor's Apology: In the last issue of the *Journal* one of the contributor's, Audrey Sloan, was wrongly identified as having attended the Mackintosh School of Architecture. This was incorrect, she in fact attended the Department of Architecture at University of Strathclyde.

KEITH ADAM

INTRODUCTION

LIVING WITH THE LEGEND

The Adam family still live at Blair Adam, the house built by William Adam for the factor of his estate. In this introductory article, the author discusses his personal experience of life at the Blair and how the family home both helped to form Robert Adam as an architect and was, in its turn, affected by the vicissitudes that accompanied his rise to prominence.

The great difficulty in dealing with this challenging topic is simply knowing where to begin, the present or the past. For me, living at Blair Adam with artefacts, portraits, papers and drawings and indeed the buildings in their 18th century landscape setting - the presence of the past is very powerful.

Of the Adam family homes; Gladney House in Kirkcaldy, The Lodgings in the Cowgate, North Merchiston, and the Blair, as it was once called; only the Blair remains (Figure 1.1). This has increasingly filled me with a sense of historic responsibility as the building, the plans for it and the vicissitudes which affected it weave a thread through the architect's story which, over the past twenty years, I have come to appreciate as significant. Some of the contents of the house - especially the water colours of Robert Adam - shed light on a man who saw himself as a picturesque hero as well as a neo-classical genius.

The presence of Robert's parents, William and Mary, as well as of his older brother John (who succeeded to the Blair) has always been strong. Their portraits hang in the dining room and they have watched over our behaviour with equanimity as we have rushed around with buckets to catch the penetrations of the elements; or even, on one memorable occasion, as huge lumps of key-patterned ceiling plaster crashed onto the dining table, spraying the room with tomato soup! Throughout these and other crises, from the eighteenth to the twentieth century, their expressions have remained tolerant and implacably unperturbed.

When people visit Blair Adam they are often surprised that it is not an Adam house and that one of its two Adam fireplaces is a recent addition It is Robert Adam's own story which can explain this.

1.1 Drawing of Blair Adam, 1736 (Photo Keith Adam)

Built in 1733 on a rocky spur of wild and unsheltered moorland, the Blair was a simple two storey vernacular building erected by William Adam for his estate factor. The grounds were laid out in the formal style of the period. Many trees were planted out in the nurseries; some coal was worked; the system of enclosure was effected, and a small planned village, Maryburgh, named after Robert's mother, was built in the vicinity. William, having become the 'universal architect of the country', was sanguinely referred to by his children as 'old stone and lime' and would have had few moments for relaxation; for we are informed that he had 'so many real and so many imaginary projects that he minds no body nor no thing to no purpose'. However, it is apparent that he would have come across the Firth to the Blair from time to time to discuss progress with his factor, Mr. Barclay, and to relax, bringing some of his young children with him.

On the occasion of these visits the male members of the family were comfortably and well catered for. An inventory of September 1745 shows that, as well as the luxury of several feathered box beds; there were 32 chairs; numerous pewter pots and nine bottles of Fontiniack, 21 bottles of brandy (3 of cherry), 8 bottles of port, 13 bottles of strong Acquavitae, 16 bottles of ale and 12 bottles of Juniper souring.

Perhaps on the darker nights William would have told the children of some of the deeds of their forebears: Duncan, one of the seven Scottish knights who bore Robert the Bruce's heart in a silver casket towards the Holy land and fought on the King of Castille's side against the Saracens; Reginald who seized as his booty on a

Northumberland raid a lady named Catherine Moubray, 'who being of uncommon beauty he soon thereafter married her'; and John who died at Flodden field.

Romantic stories like this, of castles and heroes, are still recounted to my own children today. Yet one of the stories which was passed on was about the family lands at Forfar being sold as a consequence of one forebear being a 'bad economist'. These words have always resounded in my mind as I battle with the bills for restoring and maintaining the rambling old factor's house. Surely Robert, whose speculative building projects caused the financial crisis which prevented the building of a neo-classical family house of his own design at the Blair, should have paid heed to this more practical family legend too.

The senior line of the family continued with John, son of Archibald Adam. One of the Adams, writing over a hundred years later declared, 'It is conveyed by tradition that when the family was depressed in mind upon the loss of their land, Mrs. Adam, who had possessed good sense with a strength of judgement, said to them, 'Why despond! Our sons are young and healthy, let them learn a trade'. As a result, two of them were put to be masons.

One of the masons must have been John Adam who became a Master Builder° in Kirkcaldy, and married a daughter of Lord Cranston who, in 1689, gave birth to William, their only son to survive infancy.

I am aware of Robert's romantic enthusiasm for the Blair for several reasons. As a young man, perhaps recently apprenticed to his father's office or during an interlude in work on projects at Fort George or Inveraray, Robert composed an attractive little sketch (Figure 1.2) demonstrating how he might modify the house at which John was to spend an increasing amount of time following his father's death in 1748. Secondly, William Adam had left to Robert the partially ruined castle of Dowhill, a fourteenth century keep which was situated a mile north of the Blair. William must surely have been responding to a young son's declared enthusiasm for romantically ruinous castles on rocky outcrops. Perhaps Robert rode across to Dowhill to sketch on his horse, Pearcy, which at 14 hands high, was said to be able to trot over 50 miles a day. Like Robert I have enjoyed tramping to the ruins of Dowhill, as well as sketching alternative designs and schemes for modifying a house which became, during my youth, a burden for my parents to maintain. A third indication of Robert's enthusiasm for the Blair can be found in a letter he wrote, whilst in Italy, to John:

> I rejoice with you extremely that the Blair looks so well and that you were so happy at it and I should like much to spend a few weeks there dictating ... some Italian beauty which the length of my picturesque genius could suggest ...

During the 1760s Robert would again have visited the Blair. John had been struggling against financial difficulties owing to a partner, Adam Fairholm, burning the accounts books and fleeing. Consequently in 1765 he had advertised the Blair for sale in the *Caledonian Mercury*. Along with the Merchiston villa it was to be sold at a coffee house in Edinburgh. However John was saved by his brothers in a rescue package which tied Blair Adam as potential collateral for future development speculations such as at Portland Place, as well as the Adelphi.

A couple of years later Robert became Member of Parliament for Kinross-shire when he was described as 'Robert Adam of Dowhill'. Indeed in Kinross, in the same year as the undertaking of the Adelphi, Robert stamped his mark on the locality in a little vignette: the facade of Kinross town house. On a plaque on the facade he boldly announced that, as a Knight of the shire, he had personally decorated the front at his own expense. This has been misconstrued as a bid for a baronetcy - architectural historian legend - but Knight of the shire is merely a romantic anachronism for Member of Parliament.

In the same year he designed a perfectly conceived, neoclassical house for his brother John at Blair Adam. John and he would have conversed on the siting; it was proposed that it should be closer to Maryburgh and the walled garden; and on the style of the new house so that it might become a fitting statement of their architectural popularity.

The design is signed 11th May 1772 and it was thus concluded only six weeks before the brothers were forced to lay off 2000 Scottish workmen building the Adelphi on the edge of the Thames embankment. This was a consequence of a run on the Banks occurring at

1.2. Robert Adam, Early Design for Blair Adam (Photo K Adam)

a time when the brothers had borrowed about £120,000, showing that 'bad economy' was still something the Adam family could be guilty of. This crisis broke like a thunder storm on the fortunes of the brothers causing John's estrangement from Robert as well as from James and William - all partners in the firm of William Adam & Company.

So, the grand family residence was not to be. John maintained the old house as best as he could but was forced to advertise the property for sale once more in 1786. Fortunately, no prospective buyer came forward andhe was urged by his son, also called William, to withdraw it from the market. This son was later to write 'it is a dwelling which suits us perfectly but for the great extent of the roofs'. The same could still be said today. In fact the late Colin McWilliam once introduced me to an Adam enthusiast by explaining 'Keith lives in the cobbler's shoe'.

Yet none of these other crises in the family affairs was recounted during my childhood. All I knew of Robert was from perusing his framed, late water colours which hung, one by one, in ascending rank at just the right level for delaying a boy on each step as he made his way reluctantly upstairs to bed. Years later I was to read an account of Robert by Sir John Clerk of Eldin who had written 'hardly could his infant fingers hold a pencil when he discovered by his childish productions that in a riper season he would charm the world'; and as an undergraduate we are told by Clerk that Robert 'very sedulously occupied his leisure hours in sketching landscapes'. Indeed this was a means of creative expression which continued as a strong artistic drive well into the last years of his life. Yet to me these water colours had looked like so many Dowhill castles.

At Blair Adam I further recall a small tin trunk amongst the many papers in the family archive which had a note scribbled on top of the contents saying 'various drawings/some may be by Robert Adam'. However they were too fragile to look through. Then in the 1970's I remember our greatest anxiety was the temporary loss of the 1750's pen and ink drawings which my mother had over-protectively wrapped in old newspapers, resulting in us worrying for several years as to whether they had fallen victim of a vigorous spring cleaning operation. It was a great relief when they eventually re-emerged safe and sound.

The muniments room (which was altered into a bathroom during the first phase of restoration work on the house) was increasingly threatened by some viciously spreading outbreaks of dry rot. So crisis intervention entailed the removal of the family papers and all the drawings to the Scottish Record Office. Since that time I have been very fortunate to have had the drawings conserved by the Conservation Department of the National Gallery with financial support from the Historic Buildings Council.

Since their repair it has been a great pleasure to examine Robert's drawings in more detail. They include such youthful sketches as one of the rear view of a horse and rider (as drawn from the cart behind, Figure 1.4) and another of figures in Egyptian costume with pyramid in the background. Perhaps the young genius was already dreaming of travel in far off lands.

1.3 Robert Adam, Sketch of a horse and rider, ND (Photo K Adam)

However it is the delightful pen and ink drawings of the 1740's and early 1750's which show how accomplished Robert had become as an artist of building design whilst a young man before his departure for Italy. In these drawings he experiments with Palladian form and detail which includes classical temple structure, pavilions and gateways, and also Chinoiserie gothic follies and bridges, urns on pedestals and even a couple of quite extraordinary draped beds! It is clear, not only in these earlier drawings but also in his later picturesque water-colours, that Robert is experimenting with design, style and form as he shifts between imagination and architectural reality. This is what gives the drawings at Blair Adam their fascinating variety.

There is another feature of them too, which only struck me recently as I reflected on Robert's creative skills as an architect and on why Robert had written from Rome to a friend 'I think it not amiss for a man to have a little glisk of that infinite merit he is possessed of.' During my summer holidays I read Conrad's *Lord Jim*. In the novel Captain Marlow reflects on cosmological perfection, as encapsulated in the butterfly: 'look at the beauty, but that is nothing - look at the accuracy, the harmony; and so fragile; and so strong and so exact!' It was this which helped to explain to me the meaning of Robert's particular genius displayed not only by his designs but also by his water-colours in a picturesque form; refined in later years as Robert experimented with theories of movement by drawing castle forms on rocky outcrops in landscaped settings.

But there is another aspect to living with the legend. As the direct descendant of John Adam, I have been drawn into correspondence, conferences and competitions. I have always found it intriguing to receive articles from research on the architects. About ten years ago I received one which had the curious title of 'The Idealogical Antecedents of the Rolls Royce Radiator' written by a French anthropologist who had asked to reproduce some of Robert's early gothic drawings. Around the same time, I also received one from a Canadian academic who had a curious notion about the connection between the structure of cellular form in plants and of Robert Adam buildings. I imagined that he was comparing pillars to plant stems but on returning to peruse the article which actually emerged, entitled 'Geometric form in Adam architecture', I was fascinated by his explanation of how the brothers departed from the rigid rules of Palladianism but instead reverted to a sophisticated 15th century system of proportion based on the use of the Golden Section.

Then during this anniversary year alone I have had the fortune to visit several of Robert's castles, including Culzean, where the castle is assimilated into the romantic prospect of towering cliff and seascape so familiar from the water-colours. A month later I found myself focused again on the contrived ruinous entrance to the bridge approaching the castle at Culzean when I was judging an entry in the measured drawings competition of the New Town Conservation Committee. It gained second prize.

I was also delighted to visit Seton Castle (at last) and Oxenfoord Castle, with members of the Georgian Society. At Oxenfoord I was struck once again by the fusion of building and landscape which is beautifully illustrated in Robert's water-colours. In a different way I marvelled at the manner in which the visitor to Seton is enfolded on his arrival by the curving courtyard walls. Incidentally this front was drawn with both accuracy and sensitivity to take the first prize for the New Town competition which I mentioned. Robert's thoughts on picturesque design had come to fruition in these wonderful castles. But they had surely been conceived through romantic notions explored in his later water-colours.

Yet with the limits of mortality extending even to those of genius who have regarded themselves to be of 'God's begetting' family letters tell how Robert died quite suddenly in London in February 1792 whilst he was undoubtedly still at the height of his creative energy. Although there was a great, ceremonial funeral in Westminster Abbey, he is merely commemorated there by a simple floor stone. This has always seemed to me rather a surprisingly modest memorial to a man of genius and I long puzzled over the absence of a plaque in the family mausoleum which he had designed for his father in the Greyfriars Churchyard. This is probably explained by the testy comment concerning Robert and James made by their nephew William: 'they died bachelors so there their story ends'. No doubt he was upset about the family financial crisis.

However two hundred years on it is very pleasing that a memorial plaque from one of Robert's own designs has been selected, and an inscription decided upon (Figure 9.3). In conjunction with the RIAS and the elders of Greyfriars Kirk various inscriptions were considered. It was an interesting experience to help resolve which might be the more appropriate. In the early 19th century Sir John Soane had remarked that the late Mr. Robert Adam was 'a man of uncommon talents, of amiable disposition, and of unassuming manners' which seemed to me a preferable epitaph to the proposed words of Sir John Clerk of Eldin who had declared (as if of Walt Disney) 'with his taste, his productions and his manners everyone went away enchanted'. So as you will all know Sir John Soane has prevailed.

In spite of the troubles of the Adam business misfortunes continuing well after John's own death later in 1792, the family home survived through the 19th century. The old factor's house, which William had built in 1733, remained, with its front largely unaltered as rambling extensions, additions and towers later laced themselves around the central courtyard.

Although the family have not subsequently taken to the practice of architecture (at least not professionally), they have long since forgiven Robert for the fractious despair with which he afflicted his brother. It has been suggested that the family always avoided naming their children Robert or James but this is not so; my father's older brother, Robert, died at the battle of the Somme (and my own nephew is named Jamie).

Seven years after the First World War as a young naval officer my father received a telegram sent to him on 'HMS Gnat South China station', stating that he had inherited Blair Adam but warning him on no account to resign his commission because there were 'financial difficulties'. The consequences were as complex as the difficulties faced by John one hundred and fifty years previously. The entire place including the house had to be sold, owing to debts and taxes exceeding the value of the property; consequently even the contents of the house were jeopardised. Family correspondence of 1923-25 reveals how extremely close we came to losing everything with pressure on to sell the portraits, possibly to the RIAS, only being alleviated by the sale of the Library. I often wonder how much would have survived had it not been for the actions of my father's cousin Edward, a Balliol man whose enthusiasm for history undoubtedly helped to make my father and his Australian mother aware of the necessity to save as much of the family memorabilia as possible.

In spite of this, necessity forced him into a Sotheby's sale in 1926 when the portrait of Robert, now ascribed to David Martin, was sold for £96. The Roubillac bust of William Adam (as well as portraits of George IV and Sir Walter Scott) were sold, and an oil painting of the Adelphi fetched £138. Fortunately, two miniatures of Robert, one by Tassie, and the portrait by Pechaux, failed to meet their reserve. The sale of the Library was especially sad in that many architectural source books were sold, including the brothers' *Works in Architecture*, which sold for £30, and a copy of *The Ruins of the Palace of the Emperor Diocletian*, raising in total £1,080.00. The family archive, however survived intact.

My father somehow managed to place in store the many other artefacts which escaped the crisis of 1925 and then rather courageously, or perhaps foolishly, bought the house back from a disappointed hotelier two years later. A few years on he purchased the walled garden from his aunt and subsequently the immediate environs and the John Adam designed buildings in the vicinity of the house (on the proceeds of a lucrative post with the Columbian Navy).

The occupation of Blair Adam by a detachment of the Polish army during the war did not significantly hasten the building's deterioration. But the disease of old buildings known as nail sickness of the slated roofs, coupled with the incessant drip of rainwater on to lead valley gutters and the consequent cancer of dry rot, all but drove us out. The struggle to maintain the fabric of the building had been evident from when I was five years old, one of the roofs having then collapsed under the weight of snow from an infamously bad winter. In spite of the re-roofing of William Adam's original building in the 1960's, in 1977 an ominous HBC report began, 'a thorough inspection of the property reveals such an immense catalogue of deterioration and building defects that it is doubtful if there is any one apartment which does not require some form of remedial works: the basic problem being the piecemeal development of the house with its associated unhappy solutions.' Nevertheless I embarked on a fifteen year (as it has turned out) programme of restoration. Slow perhaps, but I hope I have at least avoided the charge of being the 'bad economist', so feared by many a generation of the family.

This has not been without its interest and indeed pleasure. One of my recent excitements has been to see the old lime mixed harling patched up and the lime wash of the facade on the east front re-applied to match the orange and yellow tone of the original colour. This has brought us to the end of phase three. We had originally planned seven phases. It will be interesting to see how many of these will be completed at the end of the day. After all, Sir John Summerson, visiting Blair Adam following the two hundred and fiftieth anniversary Robert Adam conference, wrote to me to comment 'Blair Adam is a historic document of a high order and one moreover which by the celebrity of the Adam family is such that the house must be considered not merely a part of Scotland's heritage, but that of the English speaking world'. That is quite a legend to live up to!

This article is based on a paper delivered by Keith Adam at the conference 'Robert Adam: The Scottish Legacy'.

RANALD MACINNES

ROBERT ADAM'S PUBLIC BUILDINGS

Robert Adam's desire to build on a monumental scale is nowhere more obvious than in his various designs for public buildings and civic schemes. Concentrating mainly on his late work in Edinburgh and Glasgow, this chapter deals with some of his most ambitious projects and shows how they relate to the Scottish architectural tradition in form, style and scale. The breadth of Adam's vision is demonstrated not only by the designs themselves but also by his sense of urbanism.

We should remind ourselves, at the outset, of the scale of Robert Adam's imagination, and the scale of the collective imagination of the culture in which he was trained and in which he practised. A remarkable, largely overlooked drawing, which is possibly the work of Robert Adam himself, illustrates the point: this is a large, fold-out drawing enclosed with the *Proposals for the City of Edinburgh*, of 1752 (Figure 2.1).[1] If we look at this closely, we can see that it is far more than a new 'entry' to the town; it appears to be also a bridge, a 'megastructure' presaging the later South Bridge adventure. Now the reason for suggesting the author as Robert Adam will become clear but, for the moment, let us briefly look at the 'problem' that this drawing points up, whereby all pre-Grand Tour drawings and projects are presented as the work of John Adam.[2]

The historiography of the Adams is absolutely central to an understanding and re-evaluation of Robert Adam, possibly more so than any other architect. This historiography is complex, but it can be briefly summarised as the co-mingling of two myths, which dovetail into one great myth: Adam's supposed triumph over provincialism, achieved through the influence of Antiquity. This historiography allows - even demands - the characterisation of Robert Adam as a product of English provincial architecture.[3] Now when we look at the 'Proposal' drawing, it therefore presents a puzzle. From what English source could it spring? This great 'megastructure' is, of course, the product of another nation's architectural tradition, namely our own. Bizarrely, but, perhaps, typically, Adam's own country is the last place architectural historians have looked. The massive building proposed presents a theme of monumentality that we will see repeated again and again in Adam's mature work, but it is quite clear that this monumental tendency was present from the start.

2.1. Robert Adam (attr.). Sketch design for North Bridge, Edinburgh. Attached to a copy of the Proposals for carrying on Certain Public Works in the City of Edinburgh, Edinburgh, 1752 (Reproduced by permission of RIBA)

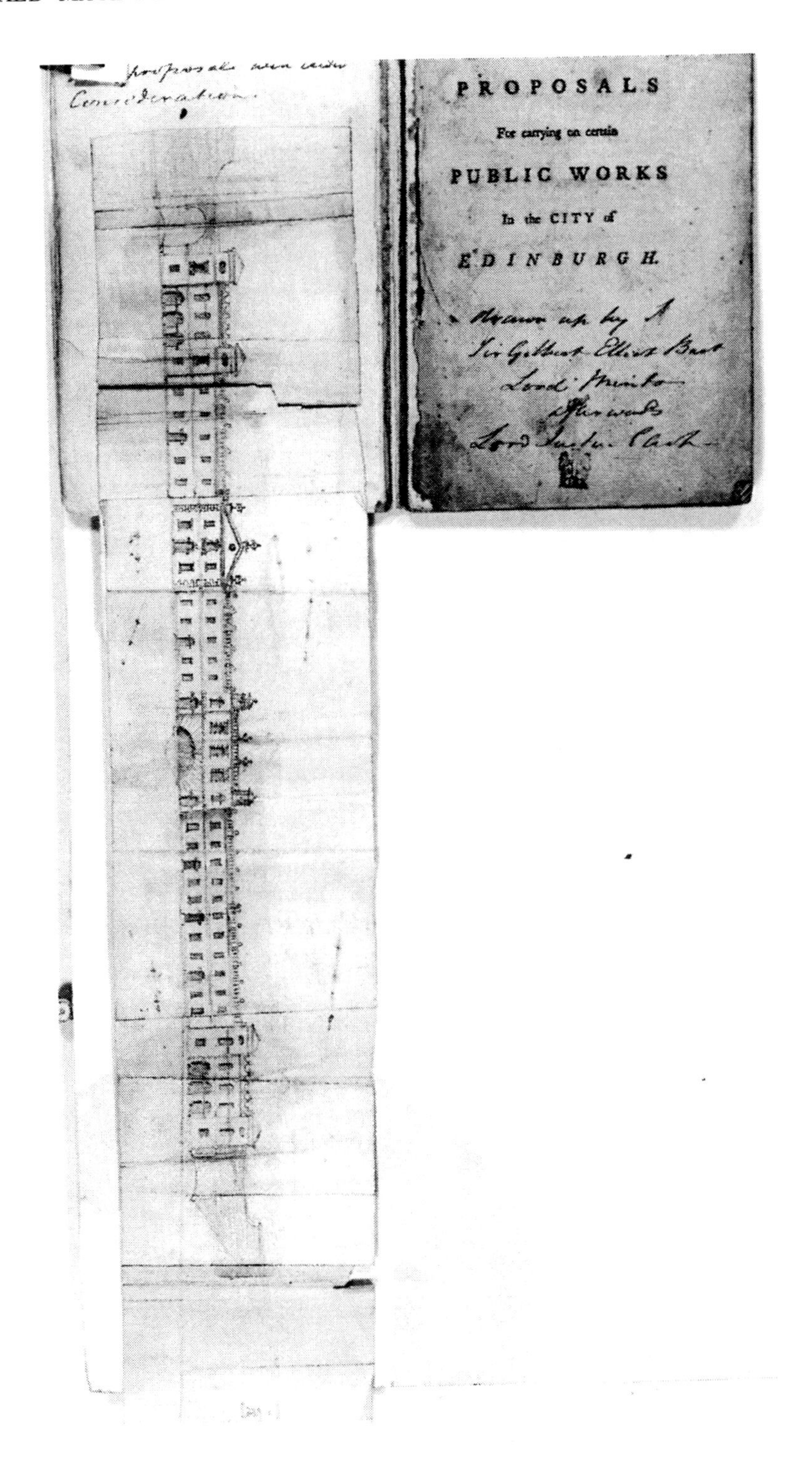
proposals were under
Consideration
PROPOSALS
For carrying on certain
PUBLIC WORKS
In the CITY of
EDINBURGH.
Drawn up by
Sir Gilbert Elliot Bart
Lord Minto
afterwards
Lord Justice Clerk

In 1752, Robert Adam was a practising architect of 24 years of age, which was, in a sense, a far more advanced age than it is now. Remember, for example, that William Burn had designed North Leith Church by the age of 24 and the expensive and daring Custom House at Greenock at 26. In 1752, Adam had been in practice for many years, and was still three years away from his arrival in Rome, and his meeting with Piranesi. Now this meeting, which, of course, has been subjected to the usual ruthless provincialising historiography, is crucial, for Adam, for Piranesi, and for European neo-classicism. Piranesi, who had rejected the advances of Chambers and all the rest, was besotted with Robert Adam; entranced by the powerful imagination of the Scots architect. Yet the epoch-making meeting of these two imaginative geniuses has been presented as the encounter of a great master with a gauche 'provincial'. Adam in his 'early' career, like his father throughout his, is presented in the sudden context of Britain as a 'provincial'.[4] But we know from the quality of the work produced in his Italian tour, that his is the work of a genius, in a powerful national tradition. In Robert Adam, Piranesi found a kindred spirit; an architect imbued with the spirit of Antiquity and with an ambitious desire to create monuments in the 'grand' manner. But Adam needed patronage - preferably the no-expense spared state patronage of the type that brought into being the hugely expensive Somerset House in London - if his mighty imagination was to find physical expression. We may still consider it one of the tragedies of history that the State which would surely have employed its greatest architect, had been abolished, leaving a yawning gulf in patronage which led Adam himself to describe Scotland as a 'narrow place'. Our 'Proposals' drawing tells us that what was lacking was not vision, but patronage.

In England, where Robert Adam set up a practice in his thirtieth year, he succeeded jointly, with Sir William Chambers, to the post of Surveyor to the King in 1761; only one of a vast number of posts created for the new 'Britain' in the eighteenth century, all in England.[5] But this position brought him no commissions of any consequence; he was, indeed, denied any significant royal favour in his architectural career.

The Admiralty Screen is a small-scale project carried out in the 1760's and, tiny though this commission was, it was highly influential. It is clear, from correspondence and from the sentiments expressed in the brothers' *'Works in Architecture'*, that Adam's ambitions lay firmly rooted, not in the private world of alterations and additions, nor of firescreens and girandoles, but in the public domain - in the widest possible sense of the term - of churches, bridges, and monuments.[6] Such commissions allowed architectural expression of the purest sort, untrammelled by the necessities of domestic life. In addition to the search for monuments, we can also trace something clearly related to the will to create buildings and urban spaces of great scale and monumentality: the tendency to 'megastructure' in Robert Adam's art. This tendency is natural for an architect like Adam, trained and practising in Scotland. The great theme of our architecture - from the tower house to the tower block - has been the unashamed love of great scale. At the time of its construction in the seventeenth century, Milne's Court, for example, must thave been one of the biggest groups of dwellings in the world. The monumental radition, which had gone from strength to strength, and culminated in the building, in the immediate pre-union period, of the tremendous power-statements of Fyvie, Glamis, Thirlstane, and Drumlanrig, achieved no public parallel. This court architecture was validated by an elite, but with no monarch to set the State seal of approval on its productions. Holyrood is the one exception. And what an exception! It dramatically re-works the monumentality of the James V work. The massive 'hôtel', which was thus created became a great national icon, and in it we might see the pre-cursor of the Admiralty screen, and of the main front of Edinburgh University.[7] This was the tradition inherited by William Adam and, thereafter, his sons John, Robert and James. We should not, therefore, be surprised to see the genius of Robert Adam re-interpret and re-vivify that tradition in a forceful court revival at the Bridewell prison in Edinburgh.

But monumentality is not only present in the public work. At the south front of Kedleston, for example, the obvious source is the arch of Constantine, and the more immediate exemplar is Salvi's Trevi Fountain of 1732, the monument par excellence of eighteenth century European neo-classicism. But there is, of course, the natural pre-cursor to Kedleston, William Adam's House of Dun, whose entrance front is essentially a re-working of the Earl of Mar's scheme for the same house.

Adam's use of the triumphal arch motif is, as we shall see, not isolated to Kedleston; it was used, for example, effectively at his re-modelling of the Paymaster General's house in Whitehall in 1771, and in almost all of the later public schemes. Luton Park of 1764 also illustrates this tendency, but in this case the monumentality is created through simple massing and the, now familiar, triumphal arch, which we can trace in Scots architecture right back to the Stirling forework gateway of 1500-1510. The necessity of providing windows was a constant bugbear to Adam. He wrote in the 'Preface' to the *Works in Architecture* almost impatiently that windows:

> render it difficult, if not impossible, to preserve that greatness and simplicity of composition, which, by imposing on the imagination, strikes the mind.[8]

It is within this context that we should consider Robert Adam's most remarkable public building, the Edinburgh Bridewell, or more prosaically Calton Gaol (Figure 2.2). It was one of the last great projects with which he had a personal involvement.

In 1791, Adam returned from England for what was to be his last, and his longest, stay at home in Scotland. On his way he spent 18th May in Manchester, where he gave 'drink money' to the porter 'at seeing the Baily prison'.[9] This standard, radially-planned prison was the work of the then recently-deceased architect William Blackburn, who will appear in our discussion of the Glasgow Infirmary. Now, the Edinburgh Bridewell was not, in 1791, a new scheme. In 1782, a plan had been made and published in Edinburgh by the celebrated Lord Provost, David Steuart and the Sheriff Depute of the County,

2.2. Robert Adam. Unexecuted scheme for the Edinburgh Bridewell, north elevation, 1791. (Reproduced by permission of Soane Museum)

Archibald Cockburn. The form of the building - very much informed by the Howard/Blackburn school of thought - was already determined when the Act of 1791, providing for the erection of the Bridewell, was passed. In a drawing marked 'plan for Bridewell', Adam is using a radial plan, apparently close to one by John Baxter for the same scheme. But Baxter's scheme is an exact copy of Blackburn's New Bayley (which Adam had paid to see) and this is clearly Adam's version of the same scheme. This plan is not mentioned by Bolton, but is almost certainly a pre-1792 Edinburgh Bridewell design. Typically, there are many designs for the Bridewell in the Soane Museum, none of which seem to relate exactly to the executed one. It was Archibald Elliot who was left in charge of the project on the death of James Adam in 1794, and it was he who built the Felons' Prison and the Governor's House, which is the only remaining building.

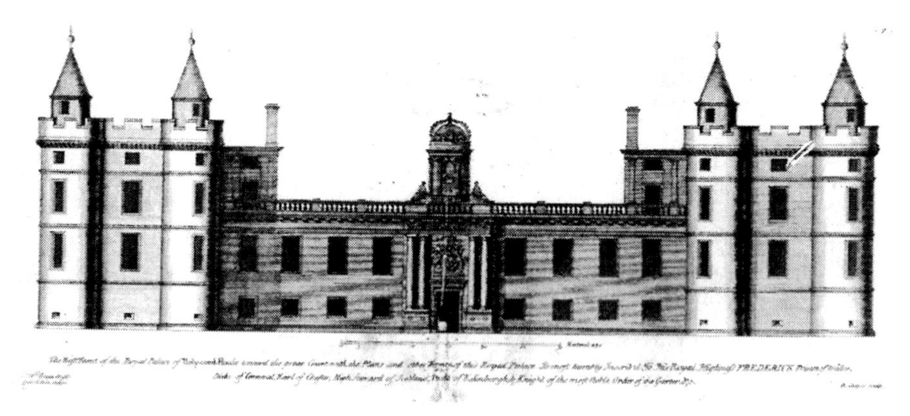

2.3. William Adam. Vitruvius Scoticus, plate 3, Holyrood Palace, west elevation. (Reproduced by permission of RCAHMS)

The massive, castellated building on Calton Hill might convincingly be made to fit a psychological state/power/order argument on the basis of its style or perhaps its location. But, in fact, Adam had offered - as he had offered elsewhere - a classical alternative.[10]

Why then was the Court Revival style appropriate for the Bridewell? George Dance's Newgate Prison in London has been suggested as a source, but it belongs more to the type of heavily-rusticated Palladianism suitable for arsenals, barracks, or other places of strength. It does not really have the required 'castle air'.

Much the closest model for the Bridewell was the James IV and V period of Court Architecture in this country; particularly the Renaissance towers of the Stirling Forework Gateway, Falkland, and most spectacularly, Holyrood, whose entrance front was engraved for *Vitruvius Scoticus* (Figure 2.3).[11]

The prominence of the Bridewell complex and its ancillary buildings eventually became too much for the people of Edinburgh. Attitudes to penology had turned full circle, and the citizens began to see its visible existence as rather like 'washing their dirty linen in public'. But why was so prominent a site chosen? As John Paterson explained:

> The building of the Bridewell on top of the Hill would give full room for furnishing a plan, partly designed, and what might be designed by you if the Provost and the Town honoured you with that employment.[12]

Paterson is talking here about the suggested entry to the town, mooted in connection with Bridewell: one of three schemes, each of which is concerned with a road improvement, with the North Bridge as the hub of the schemes. The intended course for this new road was, in Paterson's words:

> to throw an arch over the low Calton opposite the present road to Calton Hill.[13]

Given the restrictions of property relations, the vision of Adam and of the City was remarkably ambitious (Figures 2.4 and 2.5). Paterson represented Adam's interests by suggesting an alternative to continuing the 'present winding course to the top of the burying ground.', and he told the Provost and his officers that 'They had it within their power to make one of the finest approaches ... in the World'.[14]

The only obstruction to the commission for Robert Adam came, not from Baxter or Wardrop - who had both submitted designs - but from William Blackburn who, if he had lived, according to his obituary in the Caledonian Mercury, 'would have had the honour to assist in bringing forward in Scotland a system that will effectively improve even criminal law'.[15] Clearly, then, the architect was already in league with the philosopher. Blackburn would have saved his fellows 'from the lash and the cord of the hangman, punishments not more barbarous than prejudicial to society'.[16]

2.4. Robert Adam. Sketch Design for Calton Hill viaduct, Edinburgh, 1791, classical version. (Reproduced by permission of Soane Museum)

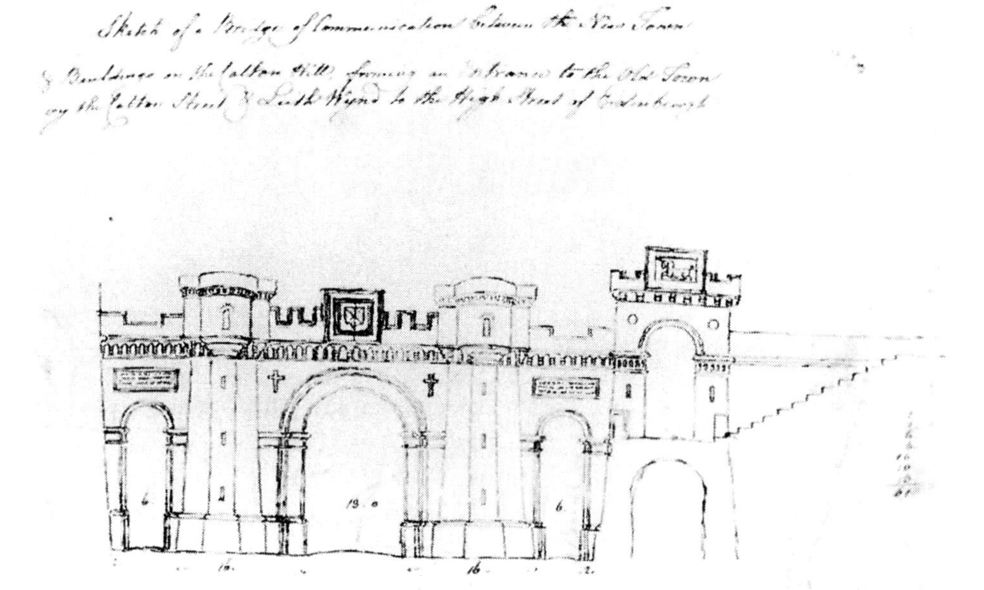

2.5. Robert Adam. Sketch design for Calton Hill viaduct, Edinburgh, 1791, Scottish Court Style version. (Reproduced by permission of Soane Museum)

The plans in the Soane Museum of the radial and non-Panopticon type probably date from between May 1789, when the Bridewell plan was first seriously discussed by the Council, and May 1791, when Adam was first introduced to Bentham's architectural invention, of which he warmly approved.[17] Bentham admitted to being flattered 'to find my gimcrack so well approved of by so able a judge'.[18]

Adam was clearly delighted with Bentham's 'gimcrack'. Not only because of its ingenuity, but also because it would perhaps allow him to steal a march on his rivals in Edinburgh, Baxter and Wardrop. Although Blackburn was dead, Adam found the magistrates still attracted to Blackburn's ideas. Adam told Pole Carew that he wanted to combine with whoever Bentham had sent the book to in Edinburgh and persuade them 'to join with me in showing them (the magistrates) the infinite superiority of Mr B's inspection principle over his (Blackburn's) and everything of the kind hitherto thought of.[19]

The executed scheme was, in fact, very far from what Bentham would have sanctioned. He later discovered that there were critical departures from his own design - for example, night time surveillance; to us, a monstrous idea involving constant illumination. Bentham contacted James Adam, who had taken over the contract on Robert's death in March 1792, presumably in an effort to change his brother's design. James had no time for Bentham, but he did not, as was suggested by Bentham, proclaim himself or Robert sole designer of the Bridewell. On 2 September 1793 Samuel Romilly wrote to Bentham:

> The plan (of the Bridewell) is Adam's and I am informed that he admits that he took the idea of it from your brother (Bentham credited his own brother, Samuel, with the original idea.[20]

There are many permutations - too many to go into here - on the basic prison formula; but in this brief account, it can be seen that it is the handling of logistical problems - which are also moral questions put into architectural form - that is so remarkable.[21] Adam's Bridewell has been dismissed as a misunderstanding, a blunder, and an idea stolen for the sake of novelty. It was none of these: it was a great building by someone who well understood the panopticon principle and, more important, could put an essentially impractical idea into practice.

Arguably, the most important of the great rush of public buildings in Glasgow which Adam designed was the Infirmary, whose construction was reluctantly supervised after Robert's death, by James Adam. The story of its committee-bound development is long and, typically, complicated.[22]

The Infirmary managers first asked the English architect William Blackburn to design their new building. He was an architect little known today, but obviously famed throughout this country and England in his day, who specialised in prisons.[23] He was on his way to Scotland to meet the Infirmary committee when he died at Preston in October 1790. A contemporary journal contained the confused report that the architect was on his way to Glasgow to design a gaol, but Blackburn's trip actually had a dual purpose, that is, to give advice on the Infirmary at Glasgow and on the proposed Edinburgh Bridewell.[24] Blackburn had been asked 'by the town and county of Edinburgh' as the leading exponent in prison design to give advice on the new gaol 'now staked out on Calton Hill'.[25] Blackburn's sudden death therefore brought Adam two very large commissions, both of which he managed to wrest from others by using all the influence and architectural ingenuity he could bring to bear on the two committees responsible for the contracts.

By September 1791 the committee had commissioned Adam and 'received plans' the estimated cost of execution of which was £8,800.[26] Adam then had to face yet more committees, this time for the South Bridge scheme, the University, and the Bridewell. In Glasgow again, Adam wrote that he met the Assembly Rooms committee, on the 15th the Trades Hall and the Assembly Rooms committees. Bearing in mind that the membership of these committees overlapped, it is a great tribute to Adam's diplomacy and business acumen that he managed to design eight public buildings and deal with eight fractious committees in the last year of his life.

The drawing in the Soane Museum marked 'Another drawing for the Infirmary at Glasgow' seems to come closest to the executed design.[27] The reason why there are certain inconsistencies in detailing is that, following Adam's death, and despite the pleas of his sister that the contract be continued 'if the loss is at all bearable', James Adam refused to take up the commission.[28] Instead he reluctantly agreed to act as surveyor, with the local contractors Morrison and Burns carrying out the work.

For all that, the finished Glasgow Infirmary was unmistakably a work of Robert Adam. James Adam's role in this case, and in most others, was to execute the design as faithfully as possible. Like Register House, the main elevation appears curiously conservative, almost Louis XV in spirit, and with none of the lightness associated with the work of the 1770s. Yet it recalls the earlier, more vigorous hybrids such as the fully neo-classical south front at Kedleston or the Doric hall at Syon. The relationship of the side blocks to the central core, which arrangement exists in all the late Adam public buildings, appears also in Adam terrace architecture, where the transition into the later, more monumental style can be traced.

Robert Adam strove after the monumental in public architecture. Indeed, as we have seen, he was criticised for it - ironically enough since he drew attention to this feature in the *Works* - at the Earl of Bute's Luton Park; Samuel Johnson thought his Kedleston would answer well for a town hall[29] and Edinburgh University was thought by another writer to be 'more like a palace fit for a sovereign than a University'.[30] On the other hand, Edinburgh Town Council had demanded a similar, monumentally grand style for the facades of Charlotte Square.[31]

That was one commission, one committee. What of the others? Adam wrote in his journal on Wednesday September 14 1791 that he met 'the Assembly Rooms committee' and on the 15th the Trades Hall committee who, he says, 'agreed to give me the sole direction and surveying and paid on account thereof £52-10/-'.[32] Most of this was achieved through John Paterson, his assistant in Edinburgh and Glasgow.

With all this successful influence behind him, the Assembly Rooms committee still managed to insult Adam by rebuffing his first advances. This had happened to him before, at Airthrey, Alva, and elsewhere, but he was, by this time, inured to this sort of attack. Not so his sister, Margaret Drysdale, who wrote in outrage to her sister that they could treat Robert Adam in this way and he 'the first in his profession'.[33]

Robert Adam saw the Glasgow work as a great opportunity to finally impose his architectural vision on the town, linked by the geometrically arranged street plan of vistas which was then being lined and regularised through Dean of Guild controls. The tenements of this street plan would provide the backdrop to the bursts of architecture which Adam was to create, at terminal points and artificially created settings. It was, in effect, a sort of comprehensive town plan incrementally and opportunistically created.

The massive public buildings that Adam had created in the architectural fantasies of his Roman sojourn were offered, in a scarcely diluted form, to Edinburgh and Glasgow. The realisation of many was eventually possible, but, in both cities taste and ambition had to be chastened with economy, and the result was often very far removed from the original proposal. Unbuilt Glasgow, like unbuilt Edinburgh, was a spectacular European city in the mind of Robert Adam.

It was this drawing together of disparate monumental schemes - the ultimate surely the Register House/Edinburgh University axis - that characterises the vision of Robert Adam. Stylistic as well as logistic cohesion is of the greatest importance in his town planning schemes, and, in the case of the Calton viaduct, this point is well illustrated. With the changing of the style of the 'Bridge of Communication', we can associate the early change in the development of the Bridewell scheme from classical to Court Revival, so that in the visual sweep from west to east beyond Register House, the style of the Bridewell, that this most remarkable public building, is picked up and used at the new 'entry' to this group of buildings at the eastern end of Princes Street, beyond the strict classicism of the New Town.

But the Calton viaduct is stylistically doubly fitting, since it is also to form'(A)n entrance to the Old Town by the Calton Street and Leith Wynd to the High Street of Edinburgh.'.[34] Adam's huge vision, therefore, goes far beyond individual commissions to a grand conception of urban planning which, in the absence of an overall commission, he attempts to achieve by degrees.

I have not discussed another large body of work which has a strong claim to be included in the definition of 'public building': these are the 'megastructures', the huge urban projects which heap use after use on top of one another. The Adelphi, the scheme for a great new town on continental, dirigiste planning lines at Bathwick, near Bath in England, Leith Street and the multi-functional bridging, shopping, and residential scheme for the South Bridge in Edinburgh presage a stunning new phase of national development of this tradition, but also recall a monumental urban past. This is a tradition, not in flight from the city through the suburbanity of Nash, but celebrating its scale and presence, even into its more remote suburbs.

ROBERT ADAM'S PUBLIC BUILDINGS

This article is based on a paper delivered by Ranald MacInnes at the conference 'Robert Adam: The Scottish Legacy'.

Historic Scotland

NOTES

1. *Proposals for the City of Edinburgh*, Edinburgh, 1752. The copy of the *Proposals* which contains the fold-out drawing is in the possession of the RIBA. Dr Iain Brown has drawn my attention to a reference to a description of a book in the catalogue of the Blair Adam library which would answer that of the RIBA copy. It seems likely that the copy in the possession of the RIBA is the one referred to in the Blair Adam catalogue. Stylistically, the drawing appears to be in the hand of Robert Adam. Another drawing, now in the V. & A., claimed for Robert Adam (which claim is dismissed, largely on grounds of taste by Alistair Rowan in *Robert Adam*, catalogue of the V. & A. collection of drawings attributed to Robert Adam, London, 1988) may have a curious link with the *Proposals* drawing. The drawing is a satire on the type of monumental architecture proposed and promoted by the Adams. It involves a proposal for a vast public lavatory, with appropriate scatalogical iconography. Now it happens that just such a deflating joke was visited on the Town Council of Edinburgh, following the highly emotive appeal for the monumentalising of Edinburgh (Sir David Dalrymple *Proposals for Carrying on a Certain Public Work in The City Of Edinburgh*, Edinburgh, 1753). we may be too prudish now to enjoy this type of humour in the way that it was intended, but it seems too much of a coincidence for the Edinburgh joke and the V. & A. drawing - attributed to Robert Adam by its former owner - to be unrelated.

2. For example the Great Hotel, Inveraray, Dumfries House, and the Edinburgh Exchange. The most recent example of this tendency is to be seen in David King's analysis of the works of Robert and James Adam in Appendix B of his *The Complete Works of Robert and James Adam*, Oxford, 1991 which begins in 1760 when Robert Adam was in his thirty-second year!

3. 'His (Robert Adam's) form of classicism, if highly polished and refined, is rooted firmly in the architectural traditions of the English eighteenth century' A. Rowan. *Designs for Castles and Country Villas* ,Oxford, 1985, p.16.

4. Andor Gomme. *Architectural History* , No 35, 1992, p.183:

> In the introduction to his Book of Architecture Gibbs avers that his primary intention is to provide the provincial gentry with models from which local craftsmen, otherwise uninstructed in designing with taste, could work. The craftsmen themselves were not expected to buy the book and few of them did. One exception was William Adam, who came to own an important architectural library.

We can only assume that if William Adam - aside from designing houses for dukes and earls and gathering material for a book - had made the journey to England along with his countryman, James Gibbs, he would have been worthy of the title 'architect', rather than 'craftsman'.

5. We are reminded here about Fletcher of Saltoun's warning about post-union public employment. See also J.M. Colvin. *A Dictionary of British Architects*, John Murray, London, 1978, Appendix 'C' which lists the numerous public appointments of the day.

6. Robert And James Adam. *The Works in Architecture*, 3 Vols, Reprint, Academy Editions, London, 1975.

7. There are many other examples of the 'hôtel' arrangement in Scotland, including the Argyll Lodging and the Adams' own Exchange in Edinburgh.

8. R & J Adam, *op. cit.*, p.54.

9. Margaret Sanderson. 'Robert Adam's Last Trip to Scotland', *Architectural History* 25, 1982, p.38

10. Castle Semple, Caldwell Castle, and Fullarton were offered in classical or Court Revival style. There is, however, a story quoted in Arnot's *History of Edinburgh* (quoted in Andrew G. Fraser *The Building of Old College*, Edinburgh 1989, p.39) that Adam had suggested that the proposed observatory on Calton Hill should have 'the appearance of a fortification' because of its position. Bentham in his publication *Panopticon* also says that his design has been inspired by that for a fortification. There was, of course, an immense amount of amateur interest in the subject of military architecture throughout eighteenth century Europe, which led to the introduction of ornamental fortifications into gardening.

11. William Adam. *Vitruvius Scoticus*, Edinburgh, c1812, plates 1-5.

12. NLS MS. 19992.

13. *Ibid.*

14. *Ibid.*

15. *Caledonian Mercury*, 9 December, 1790.

16. *Ibid.*

17. Edinburgh Town Council Minutes, 24, 1790 (Vol 117): 'it also became necessary to erect a Bridewell for the punishment of idle refractory and profligate persons'.

18. *The Collected Works of Jeremy Bentham, Correspondence*, Vol 4. ed A.T. Milne, p.282.

19. *Ibid.*

20. *Ibid.*

21. There is a considerable amount of literature on the Panopticon or 'panopticism', which became the central theme of Michel Foucault's *Discipline and Punish* (English edition), London 1975 and which clearly influenced Thomas Markus' non-stylistic account of the Edinburgh Bridewell in *Order in Space and Society*, Mainstream, Edinburgh, 1982, pp.25-114.

22. A detailed account of the building of the Infirmary, through the minutes of the meetings of the managers of the institution, is preserved in the records of the Greater Glasgow Health Board Archives.

23. H.M. Colvin *op. cit.*

24. Gentleman's Magazine, November 1790.

25. Edinburgh Town Council Minutes (Vol 116-118).

26. *Ibid.*

27. Soane Museum Vol 10: drawing marked 'another scheme for the infirmary at Glasgow'.

28. SRO GD18/4977 (2).

29. Samuel Johnson: quoted in A.T. Bolton *The Architecture of Robert and James Adam* , 2 vols, London, 1922, vol.1, p.100.

30. Nathaniel Wraxall NLS MS 3108/41.

31. Edinburgh Town Council Minutes (Vol 116-118).

32. NLS MS 19992.

33. SRO GD18 4961/37.

34. Soane Museum 2: 182 'Sketch of a Bridge of Communication between the New Town and Buildings on the Calton Hill, forming an Entrance to the Old Town by the Calton Street & Leith Wynd to the High Street of Edinburgh'.

WILLIAM KAY

ROBERT ADAM: SOME RESPONSES TO A SCOTTISH BACKGROUND

The early responsibility and superlative practical training that Robert Adam gained in Scotland under his father and older brother contributed greatly to his genius. In his mature years he found a particularly receptive audience in his native land for the emotive castle style - an architecture that was partly shaped by his early Scottish experience.

William Adam's sudden if not unexpected death on 24 June 1748 could hardly have occurred at a more momentous time in the Adam family's fortunes or for the future direction of the architectural practice. After a short lull in the domestic output during the confusion of the 1745 Jacobite uprising, a resurgence of new and revived contracts, added to increased responsibilities for many Board of Ordnance military installations, so strained the capacity of the practice that in 1745-6 Robert Adam had been removed prematurely from Edinburgh University to take his place in the Cowgate office, at the age of eighteen. Burdened by incessant worry over litigation with Lord Braco, concerning the building of Duff House, Banff, which had been dragging on before the Court of Session since 1743, and further weakened by a long and debilitating illness, William Adam had in the last year or so of his life relied increasingly on the services of his eldest son John as amanuensis. It was no doubt in connection with the recently awarded contract for the building of a new fortification at Ardersier (Fort George) that occasioned John Adam's absence in the 'North Country'[1] at the time of his father's demise when immediate responsibility for the practice and advertising his father's death fell on young Robert's shoulders.[2]

Robert's professed ambition to train as a landscape painter was swiftly consumed by new responsibilities now placed before him. On 22 July 1748 - barely one month after their father's death and shortly after Robert's twentieth birthday, John drew up a Deed of Factory which may represent the earliest formal recognition of Robert's role in the practice:

> I John Adam Architect in Edinburgh Eldest lawfull son the deceast William Adam Architect there Whereas it is Convenient for me To Appoint fitt persons to uplift the debts Resting to me at all times when my necessary affairs Calls me to the Country And I Having Experience of the Capacity and fidelity of Robert Adam my brother German and Alexander Whyte my Clerk Do therefore Nominate and Appoint The said Robert Adam And Alexander Whyte or either of them to be my ffactors ... Committing to them full power Warrand and Commission To Uplift Intromitt with charge and pursue for Discharge or Assign all debts and sums of money Principall @ rents

> and penalties Resting by whatsoever person or persons to me or my said deceast father ...[3]

There was much unresolved business of this nature to conclude. Several patrons owed considerable sums to William Adam at his death, and while John and Robert finally secured the contested claim against Lord Braco (both brothers signing the discharge in November 1748),[4] many other debts were not recovered for many years.[5] Several early deeds bear witness to John, Robert and (from 1753) James's efforts to call in these monies.[6] During the summer and autumn of 1754 extra pressure was brought to bear on debitors in the run-up to Robert's departure for the Continent. Of these, on 15 June 1754 John and James Adam were awarded £1143 14s. 3d. Sterling against the trustees for the Earl of Wigton by a Decreet Arbitrall (in which the architect John Douglas was co-arbiter) still outstanding for William Adam's work at Cumbernauld House in the early 1730s.[7] Shortly afterwards Robert, who had been attending the founding of Dumfries House, was advanced a further £1500, and in the autumn of the same year an unanticipated windfall of £300 came their way for their services at Inveraray over the previous ten years. In their pressing need for cash the brothers did not absolve familial debtors as they even pursued their impoverished cousin James, sixth Lord Cranston, for non-payment of a bond for £23 9s. 2d.

The thorough business training Robert received under his father and elder brother was no doubt of inestimable value to Robert when he made the decision to set up practice in London immediately after his Continental studies. This early responsibility coupled with a superlative practical training in Scotland endowed Robert Adam with a uniquely advantaged background over all his professional contemporaries, giving free reign to that 'dictatorial Authority' inherent in his temperament.[8]

William Adam had played a key role in smoothing the way for Robert's career. Not only did he pass on a considerable fortune and a vibrantly healthy practice, but he perhaps made a unique contribution in elevating the station of the architect above the domain of the artisan classes and set it on course as a respectable profession. Additionally, William Adam enjoyed an unusual social ease with many of his patrons, several of whom, despite their rank, were considered close family friends - a factor that was instrumental in the Hon. Charles Hope's acceptance of Robert as a suitable companion on his Continental tour.[9]

In Robert's early youth the social standing of the architect was not held in particularly high regard. When, in 1743, at the height of his architectural reputation, William Adam testified that he was 'Bred a Mason and served his time as such', he was stressing a fundamental point.[10] Yet conversely, and largely through his personal contribution to his art, William Adam stood at the threshold of an emerging professionalism which elicited aspirations to be 'considered as a person of a liberal profession and to be treated not like a Tradesman who was to give in a bill, but like a Lawyer who receives or a Physician who pays visits in order to give Advice who get their Fees or Honorarys without presenting an accompt or giving a Receipt'.[11] It was against this background that Robert's self-image was founded. In view of his later preoccupation with his professional superiority it is ironic that for the socially ambitious Robert concealment of his professional identity was at times necessary: 'Avoid putting the word Architect on the backs of letters' he requested of his correspondents during his Italian tour, preferring to be addressed as 'Robert Adam Esquire or Robert Adam Gentilhomme Anglois', knowing the exclusivity of Italian society.[12] Back in England Adam could adopt a haughtier stance: in the 1770s he and James could claim 'It is of little consequence to us, what the practice is, among the professional builders. We are not builders by profession, but Architects and Surveyors, and live by those Branches'.[13] Clearly, the station of architects of the Adams' calibre had advanced considerably in the intervening years, though it was not until the nineteenth century that architects formed themselves into a cohesive profession. By assuming this attitude the London based brothers appear to have adopted the philosophical ethos inherent in Vitruvian writings which viewed the architect as the universal man of science unconcerned with manual labour or practical application. This is of course an exaggeration, for the Adams were supremely accomplished technicians in command of a large retinue of craftsmen whose work was carefully monitored. Robert's characteristic self-aggrandisement seems to deny the debt he owed to his Scottish training which formed the very germ of his success and whose influence never completely deserted him.

His earliest architectural experience in Scotland exposed him to a diversity of styles and disciplines: forts and military architecture, classical houses, and at Inveraray a neo-Gothic castle; all of which styles are represented in his surviving youthful drawings from about 1750. The greater part of these drawings are of classical subjects - a rusticated Vanbrughian gateway in Ordnance fashion; Jonesian pavilions for Wilton House; Kentian temples and mausolea - two of which dated 1751 may represent designs for William Adam's tomb in Greyfriars.[14] Another design with familial links is represented in a small sketch for modest additions to the Blair in which Robert's proposed octagonal pavilions may be a re-cycling of his father's favoured scheme for the pavilions at Mavisbank but rejected by Sir John Clerk in 1725 (Figure 1.2). William Adam's designs continued to influence his sons. Even when surrounded by the splendours of Rome Robert could still request copies of Scottish houses, including Duff and Yester, from which to take 'hints'. It was perhaps the combined effects of early exposure to Scottish and Continental planning that enabled Robert to liberate the English house plan from the rigorous symmetry of Palladian convention.[15] Even one of his early bold strokes - the unexecuted rotunda in the court of Sion - may have its origins in a scheme for the similar treatment of Drumlanrig Castle designed by the exiled Jacobite and amateur architect Lord Mar in Paris in 1722.[16]

Robert Adam's many early Scottish drawings are predominantly designs for diminutive, often astylar houses which reveal the influence of Robert Morris to whose *Rural Architecture*, published in 1750, the brothers had subscribed. This work was still of relevance when Robert was designing his late villas thirty or more years later. In the 1750s Robert and James produced speculative and at least one executed scheme (James's Gunsgreen House) along these lines, while it also formed the basis for John Adam's work for Lord Deskford at Banff Castle in 175, the more sophisticated Hawkhill Villa, and Lord Milton's House of the mid-1750s.

Despite these youthful drawings it is difficult to assess Robert's actual contribution as a designer within the Adam office as it affected executed works. The Earl of Hopetoun, in recommending John for the continuation of William Adam's works for the Duke of Montrose at Buchanan, Stirlingshire in 1749, found him perfectly competent though not '... quite so quick as his Father, indeed very few are ...', but had evidently already witnessed promising signs of Robert's ability.[17] At Hopetoun itself in 1752 John Adam gives a brief insight into the consultative process that operated amongst the brothers, while singling out Robert's capitulation about the detailing for the main entry steps to the house after the abandonment of William Adam's intended portico:

> We are all of Opinion that a stone Ballustrade sloping as the stair does, will have an exceeding pretty effect, & we don't despair of pleasing your Lop. as to the lightness of it; and tho' it is not according to the rule, yet Bob yields to the Ballusters standing upon the ends of the steps without any base ...[18]

In 1753, while performing his annual duty at Fort George, Robert seems to have won his first independent commission for a house in Nairn for Dr Mackenzie, factor to Rose of Kilravock, the designs and exploratory notes for which are unfortunately no longer extant.[19] Generally, however, John Adam seems to have been firmly in control of the office output in these early years and while individual attributions are occasionally given in published designs in *Vitruvius Scoticus*, as for example John's Hawkhill Villa, in general, while the brothers remained together in Edinburgh, their designs were credited to 'Adams architects'. This was perhaps an acknowledgement of joint effort or a symbol of the professional and familial solidarity of the Adam office before Robert and James broke away. The contract drawing for Dumfries House of 1754 is countersigned under one hand only in the names of 'Jno Robt & Jas Adam', and while Robert was given particular responsibility for supervising the founding of that work, his role as designer before his departure from Scotland remains uncertain.

The Board of Ordnance constituted the most pressing and lucrative work, the contracts for which had been renewed to John Adam in 1748. John had responsibility for contracts at numerous locations throughout Scotland, but it was at Fort George that the greatest demands were made on the Adams' time. Each summer the brothers took turns at supervising the construction of the defences and other buildings, Robert performing this duty from at least 1750 when he made a list (in the pocket-book he had taken with him that year on a family journey to England) of items to take with him to Ardersier - architectural and history books, draughting and sketching materials including water-colours, and a 'sketch of Johnies house'[20]. A sketch by him of about this date shows a plan of the fort and some subsidiary buildings in Palladian style, but his leisure hours there were spent in sketching and painting buildings and wild landscape - the commencement of a lifelong occupation which provided a creative outlet closely linked to his late castle style.

Rococo Gothick compositions form the second class of Robert's early drawings. The brothers' interest in Gothic (for they all experimented with it) was perhaps initially inspired by their exposure to that style in the building of Inveraray. However, these Gothic fantasies may equally be a response to the contemporary fashion for eclectic and exotic sources (Chinese ornament being another) turned to partly as relief from the strictures of second-generation neo-Palladianism. The Adams were seduced by the novelty of Gothic in their youth. During his stay in England in early 1748 when he visited the Duke of Argyll about works at Inveraray, and the Board of Ordnance in connection with the military contracts, John took the opportunity of sketching examples of genuine and neo-Gothic details, and similarly Robert's 1749-50 sketchbook is full of further specimens. William Adam had lived just long enough to witness the inauguration of Gothic in Scotland at Inveraray.[21] He was perplexed over the execution of constructional details there and yet, much earlier (1732), when discussing the design of the interior of the very classical Glasgow University Library, he demonstrated a surprisingly perceptive appreciation of the emotive power and spatial effects achieved in Gothic ecclesiastical architecture:

> By entering att the end of the room you have the most Extended & gracefull prospect of the room itself and the chimney faceing you in a right manner & att a right distance By which the height & Ceiling of the room has a noble Effect, Consider a litle and you'l see what a noble Effect the Gothick Churches have when you enter att one end which you know was a Ceremony Observed in former days And when you enter att the broad side of the same Church it has not near the same Appearance ...[22]

This pictorial approach to the treatment of interior volumes is strikingly similar to Robert's later feeling for visual drama in interiors; but Adam senior had no interest in adopting Gothic as an alternative architectural style. Nonetheless his sentiments herald a change of heart towards a previously despised style; it was a change that ultimately affected that most ardent anti-Goth, Sir John Clerk of Penicuik, who, in 1739, instigated the preservation of Roslyn Chapel, Midlothian. Through its promotion by William Kent and Batty Langley, rococo Gothick, while no longer novel, was highly fashionable by Robert Adam's late youth, and it was a style (more or less affected by archaeological propriety) that endured until the end of the century. But for all Robert's early enthusiasm there was an inherent problem with Gothic architecture - it was essentially

3.1. Mellerstain, Berwickshire. South elevation. The central block is one of Robert's early castellated houses, c.1770-8, added to the earlier wings of 1725 built by his father William. (Reproduced by permission of RCAHMS)

an ecclesiastical idiom - a fact that John Clerk of Eldin is quick to point out and which we might expect reflected Adam's own mature views. It was during the 1770s when Robert's success in England was accomplished that more business began to open up in Scotland at a time when Adam was developing a very personal contribution unparalleled in European architecture - the castle style.As an architect who drew from a wide range of sources and distilled the components, the genesis of Robert Adam's castle style is difficult to unravel in a linear, evolutionary way. Many influences have been detected, amongst them Roman military architecture, Romanesque, Renaissance fortresses, the architecture of Claudian landscapes, and Scottish castles. Added to this, there is the significant appreciation by Adam for the versatile Vanbrugh who had pre-empted the style somewhat in early proposals to re-case Kimbolton Castle (1707), in 'Something of the Castle air,' relying on massing, not ornamentation for effect, and whose own purpose-built house at Blackheath appeared like a mediaeval fortress.[23]Mellerstain and Caldwell, amongst the earliest of Adam's castellated houses, barely conceal their Palladian carcasses. Wedderburn, though more sophisticated in its architecture, is transitional, having a conventional rusticated basement exactly as in a classical house. The early efforts, such as Mellerstain with strictly regular and generally rectangular forms, are simply treated with crenellated and/or machicolated parapets; and, by the partial use of Gothic ornamentation in the interior, they may still owe something to mainstream Gothic revival. Externally such efforts do not differ greatly from the designs published twenty years earlier by William and John Halfpenny in *Chinese and Gothic Architecture Properly Ornamented* (London, 1752) except for one crucial detail - Adam excludes any external reference to Gothic details, save perhaps the functional use of Tudor labels over the rectangular windows (Figure 3.1). That Gothic and castle-style architecture were in Robert Adam's mind two quite distinct categories is clear from his late adoption of Batty Langley-type Gothick for the Duke of Northumberland's Hulne Priory interiors; and notably, in the architecture of the nearby Brislee Tower (virtually

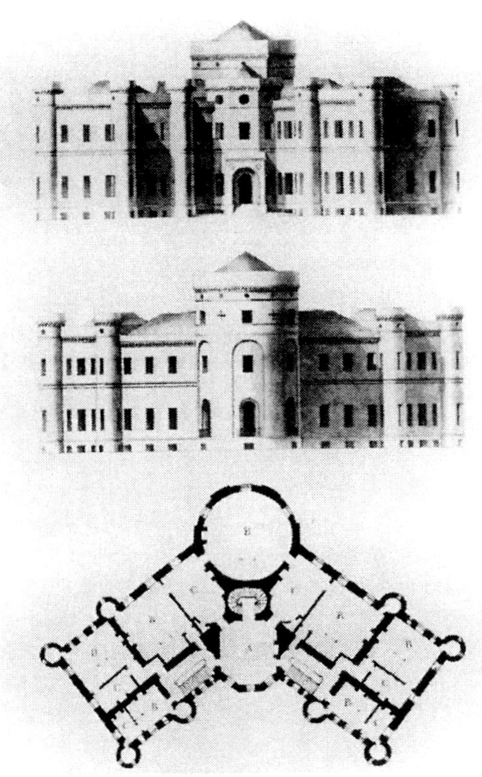

3.2. Robert Adam. Castle style design for Bewley, Invernesshire, 1777. (Plate from Alistair Rowan, *Designs for Castles & Country Villas by Robert and James Adam*, Phaidon, 1985. Reproduced by permission of the author and Phaidon Press)

the realisation of one of his youthful compositions of the 1750s) at the close of the 1770s when the Castle Style had already reached its mature form. Unusually shaped plans soon characterised many of Adam's castles (and late villas), though there had been a general vogue in published sources for adventurous shapes, again in the work of the Halfpennys. Adam made several variants of the triangular and V-shaped plan, the latter being adopted in his unexecuted design for Bewley Castle of 1777 (Figure 3.2). The inspiration for this castle may lie in the common Scottish device of the L-plan tower with an entrance in the re-entrant angle. Certainly in its general layout of circular and octagonal rooms on the apex and re-entrant angle one is struck by a similarity to Minto House, Roxburgh (Figure 3.7) where William Adam had worked on the remodelling of an old castle belonging to the Eliots in the 1740s. Minto, like Bewley, is genuinely a V-shaped rather than an L plan turned through 45 degrees: the former having a re-entrant angle of less than 90 degrees, the latter greater. Although Adam senior's work at Minto is incompletely documented, and atypical of his usual approach (though the unusual angle would have made standard regularisation difficult), yet for the sceptical there is a drawing by him for the re-entrant tower's swept dome and another attributable design for the

3.3. Castle of Mar, Aberdeenshire. One of several Scottish castles converted to military outposts by the Board of Ordnance, for which the Adams were contracted in the late 1740s. (MacGibbon & Ross, *Castellated and Domestic Architecture of Scotland*, II, p.141)

decorative treatment of the rear octagonal room.[24] Even before its nineteenth century additions, when viewed from the rear in its elevated situation Minto must have presented a very severe fortress-like appearance as a result of William Adam's minimal detailing which appears to have consisted of Gibbsian arched windows in the octagonal rear apex flanked by repetitive rows of plain rectangular openings on the facades.

Whether or not Minto was the source for the Bewley plan, part of Robert's fascination with castles and forts certainly has its roots in his early Scottish experience. Besides their work on completely new military constructions like Fort George, the Adams had inherited responsibility for the conversion of many remote, but strategically placed, old highland castles, purchased by the Board of Ordnance after the 1745 Jacobite Uprising for conversion into conspicuous outposts, from which Hanoverian forces could monitor clan movements. Originally many of these castles, such as the 16th century Castle of Mar (Figure 3.3), had been built as symbols of feudal authority. After the Jacobite uprising they were charged with a similar purpose: 'to keep the country in awe'.[25]

The revival of these castles as defensive structures involved the minimum of work to make them functional. This usually entailed the addition of bastions and outworks in conventional star patterns; and, while storehouses and barracks were sometimes added to

3.4. Base of the re-located market cross of Forfar, built by Robert Adam's great-uncle Alexander Adam in 1684. (Photo William Kay)

the old structure, there was often little remodelling of the castle itself, leaving much of the mediaeval structure visually intact. Such conversions were the very antithesis of the domestic conversions William Adam had performed on castles throughout his career, when, with consummate skill, he sought to obliterate any evidence of underlying early defensive structure. Yet, for all its Baroque dress, Duff House, his last great country house (which even contemporaries saw as a 'modern castle') is full of clever and subtle references evocative of fortified massing appropriate to the megalomaniac nature of its Highland owner, the nouveau-riche Lord Braco, who, as well as concocting a falsely ancient lineage, endeavoured to wield feudal authority on his estatesIt may be as a consequence of the Adams' Ordnance conversions of castles like Duart, Corgarff, Braemar and others that familiar Scottish detailing found its way into the castle style almost from the outset. Robert's interest in Scottish castles may have been revived when sketching (much as he had done in Italy) in the company of Clerk of Eldin, who was also a noted antiquarian with an interest in Scottish mediaeval buildings. Like Eldin, the Adams are known to have recorded Scottish castle details and these first found their way into the Adam architectural repertoire in the early 1770s when bartizans were first applied to the corners of Robert's design for Caldwell, Ayrshire. Even in the last phase of the castle style the slim crenellated towers at Oxenfoord were downward extensions of bartizans, the potential for which is implicit in the already attenuated turrets observed on native Scottish castles like Braemar. The patron at Oxenfoord, Sir John Dalrymple, was ideally placed to appreciate the aptness of the castle style as he was the author of a work on the history of feudal property and in 1760 of an *Essay on Landscape Gardening.* Both ideas are fused in his essay where he states 'as a man who is fond of great exploits or has a high regard for the spleandours of his ancestors' that 'in a Highland situation the principal house should be in the form of a castle'.[26] Such ideas accorded well with mid-eighteenth century views on the relationship of architecture appropriate to its landscape setting. To some, classical porticoes and colonnades were incongruous in the Scottish countryside, and besides, classicising an ancient house destroyed its Scottish identity and the nostalgic associations of lineage that many Scottish patrons wished to uphold, regain or assume. For these reasons Robert Adam's castle style seemed to find a particularly receptive audience.

Robert's own pride in the status conferred by ownership of an ancient property may be traced to as early as 1748 when he acquired the genuinely mediaeval castle of Dowhill, part of his father's estate of Blair which had previously belonged to Robert's uncle James Robertson, a surgeon in Culross. From then on, as a landed proprietor and son of a feudal baron, he invariably referred to himself as Robert Adam of Dowhill on formal occasions. Social aspirations so governed Robert Adam's early self-promotion that as a young man he expressed no moral discomfort in fabricating or distorting aspects of an already respectable ancestry:

> I have more than once endeavoured to convince the world that the Adams and the Robertsons from whom I come are two of the ancientist families in Scotland. I tell them the Adams are of so old a family that since the days of our first father they have been unable to trace them and that the first of them I ever heard of was one Sir John Adam who had a cross erected to him memory at Forfar on account of his great actions in war and wise councils in peace - concealing like grim death that the said Sir John was but the operator and head cowan of said cross. A good lie well timed sometimes does well.[27]

In citing the cowan of Forfar, a more lowly predecessor could hardly have been singled out as the butt of this private joke. Yet there was a grain of truth in the story. It is intriguing and significant that the ancestor concerned should be a builder, for there was certainly a long tradition of operative masonry in the Adam family. Originally of the minor Angus gentry seated at Fanno, and from about the middle of the seventeenth

3.5. Jan Slezer. Engraving of Glamis Castle, Angus. (*Theatrum Scotiae*, 1719 edition)

3.6. Robert Adam. Design for Barnbougle, Dalmeny, 1774. (Plate from Rowan *op.cit.*. Reproduced by permission of the author and Phaidon Press)

century at Queensmanor in Forfar, Robert Adam's grand-father and two of his three great-uncles were masons in the town. The fictitious 'Sir John' of Robert's tale seems to be conflated with one of these great-uncles - Alexander Adam (d. 1698) - who held civic office as a councillor and, like his older brother Charles and other members of the wider family, was a burgess of the town. Both were involved in various mason-work in and around the Forfar area. In his description of Forfar in 1684 Ouchterlonie of Guinde records that the town was then constructing a 'very statlie croce'[28] and the burgh accounts for that year verify payments to 'Alexander Adam measson to hew the stane for the use of the croce £0 14s. 6d' and, 'to Alexr Adam for going to Glames for ane stane to the Croce £1 8s. 0d.'.[29] This market cross is the earliest known structure associated with the Adam family and its castellated base with carved armorial panels survives (though without its original shaft and its unorthodox model castle finial) in a decayed condition, having been moved from the town thoroughfare at the end of the eighteenth century to its present position on the Castlehill (Figure 3.4). References to the Adam family's connection with nearby Glamis is tantalising, for it was during the period of their activity as masons in the 1670s and 1680s that the Castle of Glamis underwent extensive remodelling in a consciously archaic style by Patrick 1st Earl of Strathmore, who was 'inflam'd stronglie with a great desyre to continue the memorie of my familie' (Figure 3.5).[30] Otherwise Strathmore was not the slave of his sentiments for living in more peaceable times he omitted defensive details and sought to 'covet extremely to order my building so the frontispiece might have a resemblance on both syds'.[31] Such nostalgic preservation of earlier native features as part of a modern symmetrical layout, finds its parallel in Sir William Bruce's balancing of the old James V tower at one end of the Holyrood entrance front with another identical one at the other.[32]

These identifying features of symmetry and reference to the past are repeated in Adam's castle style architecture. Indeed Glamis itself may have provided the picturesque inspiration for his design of 1774 for Barnbougle Castle, Dalmeny, for the Earl of Rosebery (Figure 3.6). This comparison is particularly evident in elevation. Adam's massing of crennelated towers and bartizans give the impression of the forbidding and enormously complex fortified citadel, recalling Defoe's enthusiastic description of Glamis as appearing in the distance 'so full of turrets and Lofty buildings ... that it looks not like a Town but a City'.[33] The complexity of the Glamis plan is an extreme if characteristic feature of Adam's late villas and castles and are part of the neo-classical preoccupation with the ideal geometrically beautiful plan - a theoretical pursuit copiously exhibited in the competitions of the French Academy at Rome - and one reason that this design was probably never seriously intended to be put into execution.

It is appropriate that the inspiration for one of Adam's most elaborate castle schemes should be found in the very locality that his ancestors, those seventeenth century Angus Adams who founded the great architectural dynasty of which he was the final 'picturesque hero'. In the last castle style perhaps Robert was reminded of his youthful involvement in Ordnance works and, with the experience of his Continental studies saw an opportunity to develop an architecture suitable to the Scottish landscape and acceptable to the Scottish temperament; which cleverly conveyed the idea of past ages without being time-specific; an architecture that was perhaps an equivalent of how the Scottish castle might have appeared or evolved had the Roman Empire endured. Like the reality of the Ordnance forts he knew as a youth, in Adam's drawings his castles often appear as lonely frontier outposts from which unseen sentinels observe, hermetically sealed from a hostile environment. In these late castles which gave Adam much work in his native land in his twilight years we may perceive a reconciliatory fusion of Bob the Roman and Bob the Caledonian.

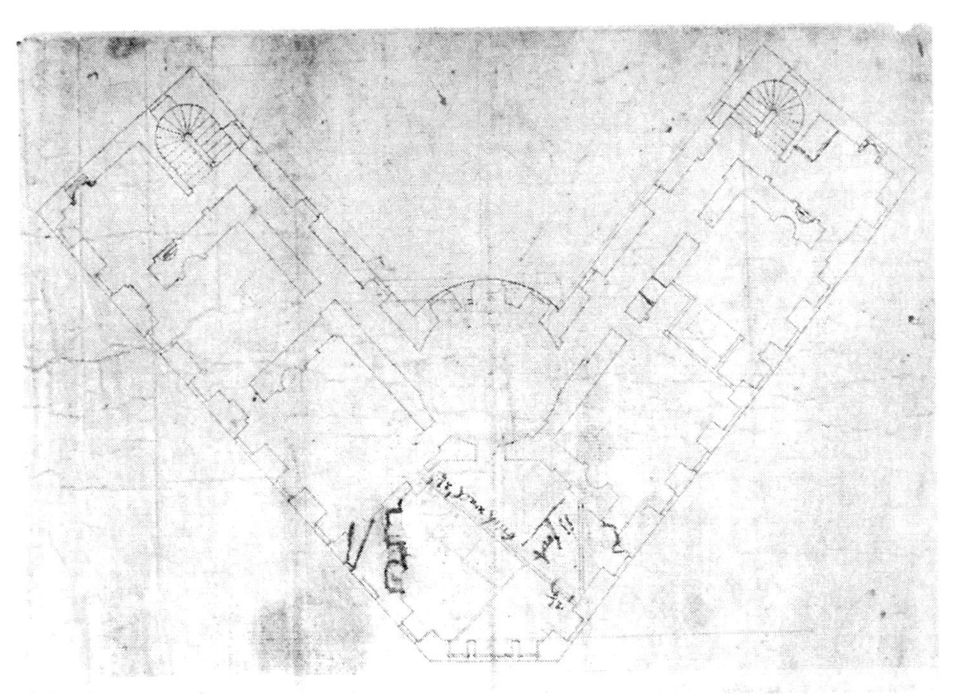

3.7. Eighteenth century plan of Minto House, Roxburghshire (Reproduced by permission of the National Library of Scotland)

This article is based on a paper delivered by William Kay at the Conference 'Robert Adam. The Scottish Legacy'

University of St Andrews

NOTES

1. SRO GD 220/5/935/10, John Adam to the Duke of Montrose, Edinburgh, 30 June 1748.

2. NLS MS 1665, f15, Robert Adam to Lord Milton, Edinburgh, 25 June 1748.

3. SRO B 22/20/101, Factory, John Adam to Robert Adam and Alexander Whyte, 22 July 1748. The witnesses to this document were the Adams' legal agent George Boswell, writer in Edinburgh and his son Thomas. A memo on the cover notes that two extracts were made out on 25 December 1765, which may indicate Robert exercising these rights to family funds after he settled in London.

4. SRO RD 13/88/135 (7 pages), Discharge John Adam to Lord Braco, 25 November 1748 (registered 28 November).

5. In the 1770s John was still pursuing payments from Duke of Hamilton for William Adam's at Hamilton work from 1727: SRO GD 31/554, Copy Report on John Adam's claim.

6. SRO RD 4/179/2, 28 August 1753, in which James Adam is the writer of and witness to a discharge and receipt concerning payment of tack duty for the Adams' continued interests in part of the forfeited Winton Estate acquired from the York Buildings Company in the late 1720s by William Adam.

7. SRO RD 2/175 ff.505v - 507, Submission & Decreet Arbitrall Earl of Wigton's Trustees and John Adams, 15 June 1754.

8. SRO GD 18/4783.

9. 'On his deathbed' the Earl of Stair left William Adam £50 Sterling 'as a memorial of his friendship', SRO GD 135/2227/32. Another patron with whom Adam senior enjoyed a convivial relationship was James, 5th Duke of Hamilton, who also acted as a witness at James Adam's birth in 1732. John Fleming, *Robert Adam and his Circle* , John Murray, London, 1962, p.323, n.3.

10. SRO CS 230/A/1, Act and Commission William Lord Braco against William Adams, p.139.

11. Petition for William Lord Braco against Mr William Adams, p.5.

12. Fleming,*op.* cit., p.173, Adam had noted that the wife of the painter Allan Ramsay was excluded from Italian society as a consequence of her husband's occupation.

13. Correspondence of Robert and James Adam with Charles Townley, 1777-9. Cited by Howard Colvin, 'The beginnings of the architectural profession in Scotland', *Architectural History*, 26 (1986), p.168.

14. It transpires that the site of William Adams' burial was an established family plot. Originally a piece of ground over it for the Greyfriars mausoleum twenty by twenty-six feet was sought. In the event the authorities granted the present sixteen foot square on 28 March 1754. (Edinburgh Town Council Minutes, City Archive).

15. Ian Gow, 'William Adam: A Planner of Genius', *Architectural Heritage I*, Edinburgh University Press, Edinburgh,1990, p.73.

16. SRO RHP 13256/65. Several of Mar's visionary designs executed in exile are based on such centralised plans, often incorporating a dome - all being variations on the theme of the plan of Louis XIV's Chateau of Marly. There is some evidence that William Adam (and thus perhaps Robert) was familiar with Mar's drawings - besides their link in designs for Dun, Adam re-drew one of Mar's designs for a Royal Palace for inclusion in *Vitruvius Scoticus* (Pl. 110).

17. SRO GD 220/5/9938/6, Lord Hopetoun to the Duke of Montrose, Edinburgh, 5 January 1749.

18. Hopetoun MSS, NRA(S) 888, temp. bundle 3459, John Adam to the Earl of Hopetoun, Edinburgh, 1 March 1752.

19. SRO GD 18/4982, memoir of John Clerk of Eldin.

20. RIBA Drawings Collection. Robert Adam's sketch-book 1749-50 p.36.

21. It is worth noting three rude sketches possibly by William Adam for crenellated doocots for the Lord Ilay's Peebleshire farmhouse at the Whim dated 1738. (NLS, Saltoun MS. 17645, f. 266-8).

22. Glasgow University Archive MS 30387, William Adam to [? Principal Neil Campbell], Edinburgh, 20 April 1732.

23. Kerry Downes, *Hawksmoor*, London, 1969, p.57.

24. There are several contemporary plans for Minto in NLS MS 13233.

25. MacGibbon & Ross, *The Castellated and Domestic Architecture of Scotland*, Edinburgh, 1887, p.139.

26. Alistair Rowan, 'Oxenfoord Castle, Midlothian', *Country Life*, August 15, 1974.

27. Fleming, *op. cit.*, p.2.

28. 'Information for Sir Robert Sibbald anent the Shyre of Forfar by Mr Ochterlony of Guinde', in *Macfarlane's Geographical Collections* II, p25. Scottish History Society, 1906.

29. Forfar Burgh Records, Montrose Public Library, *Treasurer David Wood's Discharges* for 1684.

30. *The Book of Record. A Diary Written by Patrick, First Earl of Strathmore, 1684-9*, Scottish History Society, IX, 1890, p.19.

31. *Ibid.*, p.41.

32. Preservation of or reference to early native structures is a recurring undercurrent in early Scottish classicism. As late as 1704 Alexander Edward incorporated twin towers at Brechin Castle. Lord Mar also proposed to allow to his ancient seat Alloa tower expression within his envisaged extensions to create a Baroque palace.

33. Daniel Defoe, *A Tour through the whole Island of Great Britain.* Peter Davies, London, 2 vols., 1927, Vol II, p.75. Cited in James Macaulay, *The Classical Country House in Scotland*, Faber & Faber, London, 1987, p.2.

NEIL MANSON CAMERON

ADAM AND 'GOTHICK' AT YESTER CHAPEL

The fascinating early designs in a neo-mediaeval style by Robert and John Adam show the influence of English Decorated Gothic and Batty Langley combined with a profound sense of architectural fantasy. At Yester Chapel, however, a previously unconsidered local context can be suggested for aspects of the design, underlining the importance of Scottish influences on the Adam brothers.

There is undoubtedly a strong element of architectural fantasy in the 'Gothick' designs of Robert and John Adam[1]. While the influence of English Decorated Gothic[2] and Batty Langley (Figure 4.1)[3] is evident in many of their neo-mediaeval designs, particularly those of the 1750s, surprisingly few sources have been considered in detail in the literature on this aspect of their work. The purpose of this article is to suggest that the most eye-catching feature of the 'Gothick' Yester Chapel facade, the traceried oculus (Figure 4.3), should be considered in a Scottish context.[4]

In 1750-51, ashlar was taken from the old parish church, previously St Cuthbert's collegiate church and later Yester Chapel, to provide building-materials for Yester House.[5] In March 1753, John Adam wrote to the 4th Marquess of Tweeddale to report that 'we are busy with the drawings of the old church and gate at Gifford, which shall be transmitted to your Lordship how soon they are finish'd.'[6] By the time of Bishop Pococke's visit in 1760, the work was completed. The remains of the original nave of the church had been removed, and Bishop Pococke was able to report that 'the Marquis has rebuilt it in very good Gothic taste, and it is the family burial place'.[7] The chancel and transepts of the church were retained, and the Adam brothers built a front across the crossing arch and the west walls of the transepts, creating a T-plan chapel and mausoleum.

The front added by the Adam brothers, which was applied like a decorative skin, largely followed the outline of the mediaeval church. There is a central gabled bay enclosed by angle buttresses, which are also used to define the corners of the transepts. The buttresses were originally terminated by pinnacles, but only the pinnacle of the main gable survives.[8] A parapet with non-structural corbels was added to the wall-head, the corbels being decorated with a series of classicising heads. A line of projecting cusping along the coping of the gable encloses the pointed arch which represents the line of the crossing vault. The arch is decorated with repeated foliage motifs surmounted by a cusped pinnacle. Within the arch is a traceried oculus surmounting a recessed armorial panel. To each side of this are small niches with pointed heads, and below is the entrance, an ogee-headed doorway.

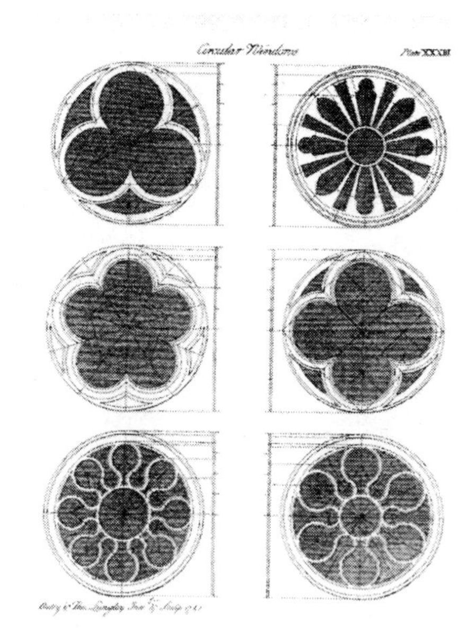

4.1.

4.2.

4.3.

The range of motifs, including the pinnacled gable and cusped arches, is broadly within the canon of English Decorated Gothic. In this respect, Yester Chapel is typical of a number of neo-mediaeval designs produced by the Adam brothers in the 1750s.[9] The elements are used in a decorative manner, creating a striking composition rather than a convincing reproduction of a mediaeval structure; it represents a form of facadism which effectively gave a folly-like appearance to the west front of the Chapel. Indeed, its central gable, which has a purely visual function, is eye-catching from both south and east fronts of Yester House.

The oculus, which has a slightly elliptical raised border, encloses original wooden tracery of elaborate curvilinear form.[10] It consists of two central loops with curved quatrefoils to each side enclosed by paired mouchettes. This design, which has been described as 'very curious',[11] is indeed without parallel in the extant buildings and drawings of the Adam brothers. There is, however, at Glencorse Church in Midlothian, a very close analogy for this highly distinctive design.[12]

The Woodhouselee Aisle at Glencorse, which represents an addition of 1699 to the south side of the mediaeval parish church, is in the form of a gabled transept (Figure 4.2). The gable encloses a traceried oculus. Enclosed within a moulded surround, its tracery design is an excellent example of Scots Revival Gothic. The distinctive curvilinear tracery is virtually identical to that used at Yester, moved through a quarter turn. Also remarkably analogous to Yester is its position surmounting an armorial panel over a centrally-placed doorway in a building which functioned as a burial vault.
The likelihood of the Adam brothers using the same design by chance, given its particular context and distinctive form, is arguably small. The fact that Glencorse Church is situated just outside Penicuik, and is close to the main road from Edinburgh, underlines the possibility that they knew the building. Penicuik was, of course, home to the antiquarian-minded Clerk family who shared the Adams' enthusiasm for the quaint and picturesque in architecture, the record or memory of which could act as a rich source for later designs.

4.1. B. & T. Langley, *Gothic Architecture Improved ...*, London 1747, pl. XXXIII. Langley's Gothic designs for circular windows bear little specific comparison with the design of the Yester tracery, but may have been a genera influence on the Adam brothers. (Reproduced by permission of RCAHMS)
4.2. Glencorse church, south (Woodhouselee) aisle. Built in 1699, it has a highly distinctive traceried oculus in its gable whichbears close comparison to Yester. (Reproduced by permission of RCAHMS)
4.3 Robert and John Adam. Yester Chapel, west front, c. 1753. The chapel consists of the late mediaeval chancel and transepts of St. Cuthbert's collegiate church to which the Adam brothers added the present west front. (Reproduced by permission of RCAHMS)

4.4. W. Maitland, History of Edinburgh, Edinburgh, 1753, engraving by P. Foudrinier of the south front of Parliament House, Edinburgh, showing an oculus of similar design to those at Yester and Glencorse. (Reproduced by permission of RCAHMS)

It is important to note, however, that a very similar traceried oculus appears to have existed in the south front of the old Parliament Hall in Edinburgh (Figure 4.4).[13] The detailed appearance of this elevation is known from an engraving by Fourdrinier published in 1753 in Maitland's celebrated History of Edinburgh. Like the example at Yester the oculus was of pronounced elliptical form.[14] It is unlikely that it survived later than the early eighteenth century.[15] It is intriguing to consider that the very year the engraving was published was the year in which the Adam brothers were working at Yester Chapel.

It may therefore be suggested that there is a hitherto unrecognised Scottish element in the design of Yester Chapel. If correct, it demonstrates that the Adams' early essays in 'Gothick' were not entirely subject to the influence of English sources and underlines their eclectic approach to this style.[16] The result is not mere antiquarian reproduction, but visual synthesis of a profoundly original character.

Royal Commission on the Ancient and Historical Monuments of Scotland

NOTES

1. This spelling was used by the Adam brothers. For example, John Adam noted in his diary in spring 1759 that the drawing room at Alnwick was 'done in a very good Gothick style of stucco'. For this reference, see J. Macaulay, *The Gothic Revival 1745-1845*, Glasgow,1975, p. 61.

2. The best overview of this style is J Bony, *The English Decorated Style - Gothic Architecture Transformed 1250-1350*, Oxford, 1979.

3. B and T Langley, *Gothic Architecture Improved by Rules and Proportions in Many Grand Designs*, London, 1747. The English Decorated style is predominant in Langley's designs. None of his published designs for traceried windows bears very close comparison with Yester Chapel.

4. Yester Chapel is situated some 150m to the south-east of Yester House, East Lothian. For a detailed description of the Chapel, see RCAHMS, Inventory of Monuments in East Lothian, Edinburgh, 1924, pp. 143-5 and N M Cameron, NMRS Record Sheet, 1990.

5. J G Dunbar, 'The Building of Yester House 1670-1878', *Transactions of the East Lothian Antiquarian and Field Naturalists Society*, Vol. XIII, 1972, p. 31.

6. National Library of Scotland, Yester Papers, Accession No. 4862, 98/2.

7. See D W Kemp (ed), *Pococke's Tours*, Scottish History Society, Edinburgh, 1887, p. 317.

8. The buttress pinnacles are visible in early photographs; a lead cap from one of the pinnacles survive and is in the care of Lady Maryoth Hay.

9. For example, drawings BA437 and BA441 in the Blairadam Collection, both signed and dated 1753.

10. Paint scrapes carried out by the architects Simpson and Brown indicate that the wooden tracery was originally painted to match the colour of the surrounding stone. Although the inner face of the tracery is rebated, there is no clear evidence that the oculus was glazed.

11. D King, *The Complete Works of Robert and James Adam*, Oxford, 1991, p. 356.

12. This comparison first suggested by the author in NMRS Record Sheet on Yester Chapel, 1990.

13. I am very grateful to Aonghus MacKechnie for drawing my attention to this feature.

14. Two elliptical windows were used in the entrance gable of the "Ha' Hoose" at Raemoir, Aberdeenshire. This building is dateable to 1715 on the basis of an inscribed armorial panel, although the tracery appears to have been restored. Simon Green drew my attention to the view of this building in the I.G. Lindsay Collection in the National Monuments Record of Scotland.

15. I.G. Brown, *Building for Books - The Architectural Evolution of the Advocates' Library 1689-1925*, Aberdeen, 1989, p. 32 and pl. 14.

16. Further discussion of Adam and the Scottish architect tradition is continued in this book by Ranald MacInnes and Aonghus MacKechnie and I am grateful to both of them for discussing some of their ideas with me.

EILEEN HARRIS

THE PARENT STYLE OR THE ORIGINAL SIN? ADAM REVIVED

After his death in 1792, and for the first half of the nineteenth century, Adam was out of favour and out of fashion. In the 1860s, however, there was a change in taste and the Adam revival was born. It was mainly restricted to interior decoration and furniture design, but was a wide-ranging phenomenon which involved architects, cabinet makers and upholsterers and covered the restoration of genuine Adam interiors as well as the creation of new 'Adams Style' interiors in country houses and town swellings all over Britain and in the United States of America. The use designers made of Adam included the re-use of original pieces in new settings, the straightforward reproduction of Adam designs and the use of Adam pastiche. So popular was this phenomenon that it was considered suitable for a great variety of settings, ranging from the cottage to the Transatlantic liner.

Adam was the man everyone loved to hate: one of the most celebrated architects of his day, certainly the most widely imitated and the most severely criticised. His detractors must be given a fair hearing, but it will be brief, for apart from being extremely repetitive, they are utterly unconstructive.

It was easy for Walpole, wielding his sharp wit in the privacy of his letters, to trash Adam's work as 'all gingerbread, filligrane and fan painting', 'larded and pomponned with shred and remnant and clinquant'.[1] Walpole's barbs may have been unusually piquant, but they were by no means unique.

Soane's assessment was more politely phrased, but no less critical. While informing his Royal Academy students of their debt to Adam for the introduction of a light and fanciful style of decoration based on antiquity, he was careful to warn them that 'Messrs Adam had not formed their Taste on the best examples of Antiquity and therefore, using the same style in Public and Private Buildings, internally and externally, they did not retain the favourable opinion of the Public to the extent expected.'[2]

That was in 1815 at the height of the Greek Revival, when archaeological correctness really mattered, in furniture and decoration as well as in architecture. Adam's classicism was too fanciful, corrupt - some even said 'depraved'. Twenty years later his style was attacked for exactly the opposite reasons by those who preferred the curvaceous Louis XIV, rococo or florid Italian style, and by the Gothic revivalists for being too delicate and worse still, too classical.[3]

It was *de rigueur* for every serious writer on architecture to declare his awareness of the defects of Adam's style. Yet, as no one could deny that he was the foremost architect of his day, a few merits had to be allowed him. Invention was the principal one, but the

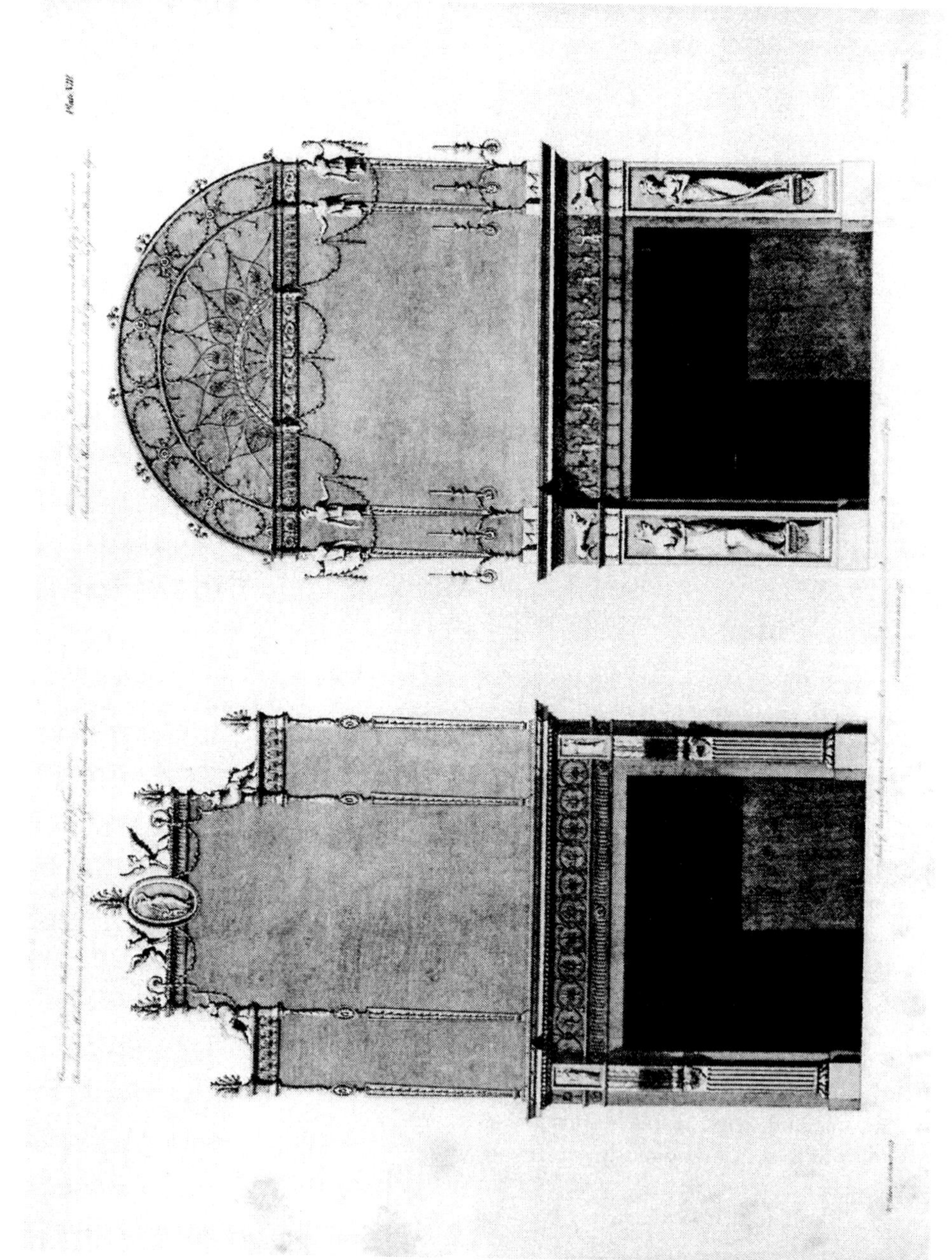

5.1. Robert Adam. Mirror Designs for Derby House, from *The Works...*, 1773. The mirror on the left was the model for the Morning Room mirror at Haddo House, 1880. The one on the right was relocated to Hinton Ampner, Hampshire, in 1938. (Reproduced by permission of RCAHMS)

most percipient assessment was made in 1831 by the reviewer of Cunningham's Lives of the Most Eminent British Architects. 'Adam's designs', he wrote, 'abound with ideas capable of furnishing far more beautiful compositions than any of his own.'[4]

It was another thirty years or so before anyone thought to test these capabilities. The neo-Adam style - known as Adams with an s and applied mainly to furniture and interior decoration - was a by-product of the larger revival of interest in the Georgian period which burgeoned into the rage for Queen Anne.[5]

The ground for this Georgian revival was laid in the mid-1850s by Thackeray's idealisation of the sensible, well mannered eighteenth-century English gentleman. The small group of young artists and architects centred around Rosetti, William Morris, Edward Burne-Jones and Phillip Webb provided the avant-garde action or rather reaction against the tough, 'muscular', brightly coloured French Gothic style favoured by their elders, as well as the meaningless and heavy imitations of the French pseudo-classical and Louis XIV styles.

What they wanted was the exact opposite of what they had - delicacy, lightness, pale colours, gentlemanly refinement, classical restraint - the very things that Adam had been criticised for - qualities which were now associated with Englishness.

There was a conscious mixture of nationalism and eclecticism in their taste. The idea of being committed to one style did not appeal to them. Style was equated with copyisms and reproduction which were deeply mistrusted. Adam was praised by J. Alden Heaton in 1889 for not adhering to the 'false standards set up by a pretended admiration of classic work on the one hand and an extravagant desire to follow all the excesses of the French Renaissance on the other.'[6]

Terms like French Renaissance, Rococo, Empire, Georgian, Queen Anne, Chippendale, Sheraton, Italian, Louis Quatorze, Quinze and Seize were bandied about with 'charming indifference to the trammels of dates'. In 1878 Mrs Haweis, the author of several books on beauty and decoration, related a tale of 'some really cultivated folks' who showed her a 'French Mirror (Louis XIV)' which they called Queen Anne, 'Empire', you-know 'genuine' Chippendale.'[7] Bolton had a similar experience in 1926 when a French visitor described his Adam room at the Wembley exhibition as Rococo-Empire. That to him was as understandable as an English student's description of the work of Percier and Fontaine as 'washed out Adam'.[8]

Before examining examples of the Adam revival, I must very briefly discuss its principal source, the *Works in Architecture*. In 1822, Priestley and Weale, wanting to capitalise or at least recoup on their purchases at the Adam sale in 1821, published rejected plates as a third volume of the *Works*. Interest in Adam was then at such a low ebb that not only did this publication go unnoticed, but Priestley and Weale also had to abandon their advertised proposals to publish an atlas folio of thirty plates of 'Architectural Remains in

Rome, Pola and Naples' made under Adam's direction, as well as a memoir of the lives of the brothers.[9]

Batsford was more cautious. They waited until 1880 when the Adam revival was about fifteen years old before publishing a selection from the *Works* of twenty six plates of the most notable interiors - Kenwood, 20 St. James's Square, and Derby House. This had a second edition in 1901.

Meanwhile, Heaton reproduced a further selection in his general book on *Furniture and Decoration in England during the Eighteenth Century* published between 1889 and 1892. In 1900 an unreduced facsimile was published in Paris. Its effects have yet to be explored.

In addition to Adam's published designs there was a book of *Designs for Ceilings*, published in 1776 by George Richardson, who began as a draughtsman in the Adam office and accompanied James on the Grand Tour. Apart from three English editions, Richardson's book had two New York reprints in the 1920s.

Finally, let us not forget how much the making of neo-Adam ceilings was facilitated by the extensive collection of moulds made during Adam's lifetime by the enterprising firm of plasterers, George Jackson and Company, from which casts could be purchased and indeed still can.

The earliest specimens of the neo-Adam style that I have found are the pieces by Wright and Mansfield exhibited at the International Exhibition in London in 1862. Ironically, the introduction to the catalogue of that exhibition by F.T. Palgrave dismissed classicism as 'galvanised pedantry', and declared 'Gothic ... best'.

Wright and Mansfield were certainly not pedants. They began as assistants to Jackson and Graham, the most important and best known Victorian cabinet-making firm, working mainly in the French manner, and then set up on their own in Great Portland Street as Adams specialists. I wonder whether their proximity to Portland Place - the heart of metropolitan Adam country - influenced their preference for his work. To what extent were they employed to restore and refurnish genuine Adam interiors in the neighbourhood? They later moved up-market to Bruton Street where they carried on a 'successful business of a high class and somewhat exclusive character'.[10]

Their stated aim was 'to avoid production (meaning reproduction) or copy of any foreign period and to illustrate English art in every respect'. No one would call their specimens of so-called 'Art Manufacture' - the details of which were said to be 'gleaned from the works (with a small w) of Messrs Adelphi Adam' - reproductions, although some, with a patina of age, might be mistaken for the real thing. First, a few words about Wright and Mansfield's most famous piece of furniture, the towering cabinet which was awarded top honours at the Paris International Exhibition in 1867 and promptly purchased by the

5.2 Wright & Mansfield. Drawing Room, Guisichan House, Invernesshire. (Reproduced by permission of RCAHMS)

South Kensington Museum. It was designed by a Mr. Crosse, possibly the architect, Edward Crosse. Inlaid Wedgwood medallions - also used on the 1862 chimney-piece - though not characteristic of genuine Adam furniture, became closely associated with it, possibly via eighteenth-century French imitations.

Wright and Mansfield's success at the 1867 exhibition must have brought them many patrons. Among the first was Sir Dudley Coutts Marjoribanks, later Lord Tweedmouth, a banker, MP and celebrated collector of French furniture and paintings, and Wedgwood jaspar ware. Brook House in Park Lane, built for Marjoribanks by T.H. Wyatt in 1867, is said to have been furnished by Wright and Mansfield, but judging from photographs taken before its demolition, the interiors, like the exterior, were in the French style.

Guisichan, the Highland sporting estate in Invernesshire where Sir Dudley kept his Wedgwood collection (now in the museum at Port Sunlight), was unmistakably Adamesque as early photographs of the drawing room show (Figure 5.2). Here we not only have 'Adams' furniture but also an Adamesque ceiling and wall decorations inset, wherever possible, with Wedgwood plaques. Overall and in detail the effect is more robust and busy than original Adam work, and not as well integrated. The *torchères*, chimney-glass, and *girandoles* are reminiscent of the 1862 exhibition pieces.[11]

In 1877 Marjoribanks' daughter, Ishbel married the 7th Earl (later 1st Marquess) of Aberdeen, whose family seat, Haddo House in Aberdeenshire, built by William Adam in 1732 for the 2nd Earl, was in need of extensive renovation.[12] The architectural work was carried out by the leading Scottish architect, C.E. Wardrop and the interior decoration and furnishing was entrusted to Wright and Mansfield whose work was well known to

Countess Ishbel. This was their most extensive and important commission, and its assured survival in the care of the National Trust for Scotland is a great blessing.

In 1880 all the reception rooms were given Adamesque ceilings. The one in the Morning Room is painted in pastel colours that were associated with Adam and were fashionable as well (Figure 5.3). The chimney-glass is inspired by Adam's engraved design for the first drawing room at Derby House (Figure 5.1 [left]). The ceiling and cornice of the dining room are, I think, particularly convincing (Figure 5.4).

One can recognise in the drawing room the rams' headed *torchères* supporting Greek style vases that were in the drawing room at Guisichan. They were probably brought here after the sale of the house in 1908 and the second Lord Tweedmouth's death a year later.

Finally the great library (Figure 5.5), which is the most distinctive room, not just for its ceiling and architectural bookcases - both faintly reminiscent of Adam's library at Croome Court - but principally for its ebony and cedar wood writing table inlaid with blue and white Wedgwood medallions and its pair of chimney-pieces inlaid with green jaspar plaques. The latter were probably a gift from the first Lord Tweedmouth, copied from an eighteenth-century original in his collection. The painted screens en suite with the writing table are what might be called Japanese Adams. The table is unmistakably Victorian in shape and composition, though made up of recognisable Adam motifs - rams' head capitals, swags and medallions.

No doubt there are other specimens of Adam revival furniture by Wright and Mansfield waiting to be rediscovered. However, it is unlikely that any interiors will be found as complete and well maintained as those at Haddo. Haddo is proof of the 'high class and exclusive character' of Wright and Mansfield's business.

There were several other firms who also supplied 'Adams' furniture, though not as a speciality. One of these was James Shoobred and Company, one of London's earliest department stores. Shoobred was a manufacturer and retailer who supplied everything for the home. His shop on Tottenham Court Road was a symbol of commercial success. There, the prosperous upper middle classes could buy fashionable Adams mirrors or a complete Adams style bedroom. What distinguished them as Adams were arabesque panels incorporating medallions, vases, anthemion, and swags - especially the latter.[13]

5.3. Wright & Mansfield. Morning Room, Haddo House, Aberdeenshire. 1880. The renovation of this William Adam house was carried out by C.E. Wardrop with the interior decoration entrusted to this fashionable London outfit. (Permission to reproduce from RCAHMS)

5.4 Wright & Mansfield. Dining room ceiling, Haddo House, Aberdeenshire, 1880. (Reproduced by permission of RCAHMS)

5.5 Wright & Mansfield. Great Library at Haddo House, 1880. (Reproduced by permission of RCAHMS)

5.3.

5.4.

5.5.

Messrs. Gillow of Lancaster and Oxford Street was a better known firm of furniture makers and upholsterers, whose works appeared in all the major exhibitions where they attracted attention as well as awards. One of their most successful creations was the octagonal boudoir in the Adams style which Gillow exhibited in the Princess of Wales Pavilion at the Paris Exhibition in 1880. A lithograph was published in 1881 by Colonel Sir Robert Edis, soldier, architect, prolific writer and arbiter of taste to whom Bolton was articled from 1884 to 87.[14] The room itself was re-erected in Gillow's Oxford Street showrooms. The Adam spirit seems dilute compared to the rooms at Haddo which are exactly the same date, but perhaps this is the nature of exhibits. In any case, the room aroused considerable interest in Paris.

It is interesting to see Gillow's 1880 exhibit alongside the Adam room they showed at the International Exhibition at St. Louis in 1904, when the French were showing Art Nouveau. Though the progress in twenty four years is by no means great, there is a discernible streamlining, simplification and reduction of scale.

There were two more early twentieth-century Adam style rooms in Gillow's Oxford Street showrooms. A bedroom in the Adams style, with Queen Anne and Sheraton style furniture, and a quite grand music room which had a suite of oval back tapestry-covered chairs not unlike those in the tapestry room at Osterley.

Frederick Litchfield and Company was another high class firm that supplied Adam style furnishings and fittings. One of their Bruton Street showrooms displayed Adam mantlepieces. Another showroom was decked out as a boudoir with reproduction Angelica Kauffmann paintings. It was designed by the society architect, W.H. Romaine-Walker who worked for Rothschilds and Duveens and was mainly interested, as they were, in French interiors. The intervention of an architect resulted in something quite convincingly Adamesque, a pastiche but not a copy.

The *Illustrated History of Furniture* published by Frederick Litchfield in 1892 and reissued many times over must have given a stamp of authority if not a direct commercial boost to this revival antiques. The same can be said of the books on furniture published by the decorator/dealer Francis Lenygon and others in the early 1900s. But this is a subject in itself.

On the subject of architect-designed Adam interiors, I want to briefly consider three rooms: first the sitting room in the Royal Suite at Claridge's Hotel designed by the architect of Harrod's, C.W. Stephens, around the turn of the century. As in Adam's own work, the style of the ceiling is carried into all the architectural features including the grate which is quite like one advertised in *Architectural Review* in 1899.

Not far away at 88 Brook Street are two rooms designed in 1909 by Mewes and Davis of Ritz Hotel fame for the Honourable Henry Coventry whose great great grandfather was Adam's patron at Croome Court. Though now furnished with computers, they are still intact, on the ground floor where it was considered polite to have discreet English rooms, reserving the more showy French style for the drawing room upstairs. Whether family tradition played any role in the choice of the Adam style here is a matter for speculation.

There is no doubt, however, that it governed the remodelling of my third example, Manderston in Berwickshire, between 1901 and 1905 for Sir James Miller, whose wife was the daughter of Lord Curzon of Kedleston. Miller's architect was John Kinross who had been in Wardrop's office. The firm of Charles Mellier and Company of Albemarle Street was employed to bring the spirit of Adam - and Kedleston in particular - to bear at Manderston. Mellier had decorated Miller's London house, 45 Grosvenor Square in 1897 in the most fashionable French style mixed with a dash of Adams.

Unlike the interiors we have seen at Haddo and elsewhere, the Adam quotations at Manderston are specific and easily identified, though the pastiche is clearly of its period. The hall chimney-piece, complete with plasterwork above and basket grate below, is copied from the hall at Kedleston, and the hall passage has a ceiling from the hall at Syon, generic Adam classical urns and pedestals, and, at the far end, a lunette from the second drawing room at Derby House. The ball room ceiling is copied from the dining room at Kedleston. The inset paintings are different and the colour is more vivid - a primrose yellow ground with pale blue bands and frieze, and the stucco work picked out in white. The dining room ceiling, which was the last to be done, is not a copy, but an original composition of Adam motifs.[15]

The architectural decoration was done by the Edinburgh firm of Scott Morton who, at that time, were also executing neo-Adam interiors designed by Balfour Paul for the Marquess of Bute's genuine Adam house in Charlotte Square.

This seems an opportune moment to introduce an original composition made up of original Adam pieces rescued from demolished buildings and put together at Hinton Ampner, Hampshire, a Victorian house Georgianized in 1938 for the writer and collector of Regency furniture, Ralph Dutton.[16] Lord Gerald Wellsley and Trenwith Wills were the architects, Ronald Fleming was the decorator. The ceiling was designed by Adam for 38 Berkeley Square, the London house of Robert Child of Osterley. Dutton bought it at Christie's in 1939 after Bolton had failed to convince the V & A to have it. The mirror above the sideboard was originally over the chimney-piece in the second drawing room at Derby House (Figure 5.1 [right])). The arched upper part was also the source for the overmantle mirror in the neo-Adam drawing room installed in 44 Grosvenor Square in 1930 by Lord Illingworth.

Mr and Mrs Basil Ionides - he an architect and she a collector of eighteenth-century furniture and china - also used original Adam fittings, including doors from 38 Berkeley Square, in the reconstruction of Buxted Park, Sussex after it was gutted by fire in 1940. Their Adamish library decorated in the 1930s - with a pair of Adam period tables in the centre of the room - was reconstructed as a saloon, with genuine Adam plaques from a house in the Adelphi over Adam style door cases. The carpet is also Adam style, but of what date I do not know. Nor do I know whether the silver basket grate is really a rare survival from the Adam period as claimed or a revival creation.

Manderston, Haddo and the numerous Mayfair interiors all support Heaton's criticisms of Adam's work, that it was 'designed entirely for rich people' and was therefore 'deprived' of 'that all-round adaptability which must be the characteristic of a really vital style, which is to become traditional.'[17] The only saving grace, as far as he was concerned, was the ability of Adam's ornament to be executed cheaply in papier mache and plaster, or even with paint and stencil, like the 1909 drawing room door picked out in 'newly invented' silver aluminium paint manufactured by Thomas Parson and Sons.

Whether a really vital, traditional style will ever be found, or is even wanted, is debatable. The Georgian-Adam-Regency conglomerate is as good a contender as any. And as for bringing Adam into the houses of what Heaton called 'burghers' - Heals and Company managed to do that with inexpensive wood, streamlining and plain white paint. Their Colonial Adam bedroom suite is very well mannered but hardly ritzy. Much the same could be said of the Edwardian olde-worlde Georgian inglenook at Redhill in Headingly, designed in 1903 by the arts and crafts architects, Francis Bedford and Sydney Kitson. Every inglenook has to have an outsize, yawning chimney-piece, but, as they proved with great ingenuity, it needn't necessarily be simple dark oak. It could be ornate white Adams.

Bolton is eponymous in the world of architectural history with two invaluable volumes about Adam published in 1922. Few are familiar, however, with the Adam room he designed for the International Exhibition at Wembley in 1925. It represents, in his own words, 'the way in which a room of the fixed dimensions of twenty four feet wide by thirty six feet long and fifteen feet high may be treated in accordance with [Adam's] ideas of proportion, decoration and colour.'[18] The only reproductions here were circular medallions in the ceiling and frieze, and a tablet in the chimney-piece. Apart from the furniture and other props lent by dealers, everything was designed by Bolton himself, including the carpet especially woven by Wiltons. The painted wall panels, which were meant to convey an idea of Adam's tapestry rooms, depict five of his masterpieces: the Adelphi Terrace, the bridge at Syon, the Osterley portico, the Scottish Record Office and the Earl of Derby's fete pavilion at the Oaks.

Just as Adam brought everything into his schemes, so Bolton thought fit to include five figures made by Louis Tussaud and dressed in valuable contemporary costumes. Not any old figures - but ones with Adam connections, however slight: Dr Johnson accompanied by Boswell and Mrs Thrale, Garrick, and Fanny Burney.

It is difficult to determine what effect Bolton's exhibit might have had. My guess is very little. Certainly a lot less than Wright and Mansfield and Gillow's exhibits. By 1925 the Adam revival had been going for about sixty years and was showing no signs of letting up.

The Adam revival was also popular in the United States. A number of houses appear to have transplanted from, say, Portland Place. One, the corner of Park Avenue and 68th Street - the Mayfair of New York - was built in 1911 for Percy Pyne by McKim, Mead and White. It is the last Georgian-Federalist residence by the celebrated firm, whose principal work in that idiom was the restoration of the White House in 1902. Mr Pyne's drawing room ceiling is so very close to Adam's design for the Duchess of Bolton's dressing room that one must conclude either that it was copied from the drawings at the Soane, or more likely, that it was rescued from Bolton House on the east side of Russell Square, when it was demolished.

There seems to me to be some relationship between the drawing room ceiling in the Pyne house and the carpet in the library in the Larz Anderson house in Washington, built by the Boston architect, Arthur Little in partnership with Herbert Brown, around 1905. Maybe it too came from Bolton House. On the other hand, the library ceiling looks like a Little and Brown Adam-style design.

America has a rich variety of rescued and revival Adam to offer. However, I am afraid all I can offer are a few examples and very sketchy information. There is a world of difference between the Adams library, for which the designer, James Thompson was awarded a prize in 1891, and Ogden Codman's sophisticated design for the library in Eban Howard Gay's house on Beacon Street in Boston in 1900. The style is Adam/Empire with the emphasis on Empire which Codman preferred. Much the same can be said of the drawing room and music room where, however, the style of the furniture is clearly Chippendale.

The New York architect, Mott Schmidt, though unheard of in this country, is well known to American architectural historians as one of the leading Adam revivalists. The colour illustrations in the recent monograph on Mott Schmidt vouch for the absence of colour in American Adam interiors that led to the publication in 1928 of colour lithographs of water-colours made by Gerald and Betty Geeblings from Adam drawings at the Soane.[19]

Finally, the swagger cigar store and theatre ticket agency in the Hotel Cadillac in the heart of the theatre district, on Broadway and 43rd Street which dates from 1907 and the more refined white and gold Adam style cabin on the Titanic completed in 1912 bear witness to the wide diffusion of the Adam style.

This chapter is based on a paper delivered by Eileen Harris at the conference 'Robert Adam: the Scottish Legacy'.

NOTES

1. Walpole to Mann, 17 April 1775; Walpole to Wm Mason, 14 Feb. 1782. *H. Walpole, Correspondence*, Yale ed., XXIV, p. 102; XXIX, p. 84.

2. Sir J. Soane, *Lectures on Architecture*, ed. A.T. Bolton, 1920, Lecture XI, 16 March 1815, p. 172.

3. E. Harris, *The Furniture of Robert Adam* , London, Alex Tiranti,1963, ch. 4.

4. J. Swarbrick, *The life, work and influence of Robert Adam and his brothers*, being the RIBA Prize Essay for 1903, p. 20.

5. On the Georgian revival see M. Girouard, *Sweetness and Light the 'Queen Anne' Movement 1860-1900*, Oxford, Clarendon Press, 1977; and C. Wainwright, 'The Dark Ages of art Revived or Edwards and Roberts and the Regency Revival', *The Connoisseur*, June 1976, pp. 95-105.

6. J.A. Heaton, *Beauty and Art* , 1897, p. 194.

7. Mrs. Haweis, *The Art of Decoration*, 1881, p. 42.

8. A.T. Bolton, 'The Furniture of Robert and James Adam' typescript of a lecture at the Geffries Museum, 18 March 1926, Soane Museum.

9. A.T. Bolton, 'Robert Adam, FRS, FSA Architect to King George III And to Queen Charlotte As A Bibliographer, Publisher, And Designer of Libraries'. Paper read before the Bibliographical Society on Jan. 15 1917.' (1919), pp. 66-7.

10. F. Litchfield, *Illustrated History of Furniture*, 4th ed., 1899, p. 236.

11. D. Fraser, *A History of Guisichan* , 1990.

12. C. Hussey, 'Haddo House, Aberdeenshire', *Country Life*, 18 August, 25 August 1966, pp. 378-81, 448-52. I. Gow, 'Victorian Splendour at Haddo House', *Scotland's Heritage*, Spring 1992.

13. There is a thesis on the firm of Shoolbred by Sophia De Falbe, 1985, Victoria & Albert Museum.

14. R.W. Edis, *Decoration and Furniture of Town Houses*, 1881, pl. 18. About Edis, see S. Neale, 'An Architect Presents Arms', *Country Life*, 14 Nov. 1985, pp. 1570-2.

15. C. Aslet, 'Manderston, Berwickshire', *Country Life*, 15 Feb., 22 Feb., 1 March 1979, pp. 390-3, 466-9, 542-5.

16. C. Hussey, 'Hinton Ampner, Hampshire', *Country Life*, 7 Feb. 1947, pp. 374-7; 11 June 1965, pp. 1424-8.

17. Heaton, *op. cit.*, p. 196.

18. A.T. Bolton, 'The Adam Room at Wembley, 1925'. *Architectural Review*, 1925.

19. M.A. Hewitt. *Mott Schmidt*, 1991; G.K. Geeblings, *Color Schemes of Adam Ceilings*, New York, 1928.

IAN GOW AND JAMES SIMPSON

8 QUEEN STREET EDINBURGH: RESTORING AN ADAM HOUSE

In Adam's bicentenary year the restoration of one of his most important Edinburgh town houses was brought to completion. This paper explains the painstaking process which brought this about.

With one or two exceptions, the houses of Edinburgh's first New Town are handsome essays by builders. No. 8 Queen Street is an outstanding exception because it was designed by Robert Adam in 1770-1771 for Lord Chief Baron Ord. Although conceived on the grandest scale with five rather than the conventional three bays, it was to serve as the model for future New Town houses until Adam himself supplied a yet more ambitious pattern with the palace fronts of Charlotte Square in 1791.

The facade of No. 8 was a particular favourite of the late Colin McWilliam for whom the elegant band of 'Vitruvian' scroll ornament was likened to a well matched tie on an understated suit. The interior, by contrast, could only disappoint. Although there were two fine ornamental ceilings in the first floor drawing rooms and two original, although displaced, statuary marble chimney-pieces, all to Adam's design, the building had 'lost its internal unity'. The most dispiriting feature of the interior was a result of the insertion of a lift-shaft in the centre of the stairwell at the heart of the house. This drastically impaired the penetration of light down from the stair's sky-light. The effect was more like the common stair of a tenement rather than the overture on Adam's architectural progress to the first floor reception rooms.

No. 8 has been the property of the Royal College of Physicians since 1868. It was acquired primarily for its vacant back green which permitted the erection of Bryce's new library which was an extension of their adjacent voluptuous headquarters at No. 9, designed by Thomas Hamilton in 1844. They had no immediate use for No. 8 which was let to a series of tenants. In 1955, however, their architect Sir William Kininmonth carried out a partial renovation of the house creating a new reading room in Adam's large drawing room on the first floor.

The recent restoration was a result of a report on the College's Queen Street properties prepared by Simpson and Brown, the Edinburgh architects, in 1988. The aim was to put all the buildings into good order, rationalise their use and consider their presentation. No. 8 emerged as a priority partly because of a consciousness of Robert Adam's forthcoming Bi-Centenary. The Historic Buildings Council gave their enthusiastic support to the restoration of No. 8 because of its importance and insisted on the removal of the lift-shaft and the reinstatement of the back staircase. Because the architectural form of the house still remained so true to Adam's intention they were also willing to support the reinstatement of missing decorative features to complete the

6.1. Robert Adam. Front Elevation, 8 Queen Street, Edinburgh,1770-71.
(Reproduced by permission of Soane Museum)

integrity of the design, rather in the way that one might replace a missing modillion in a cornice or rebuild a missing house in a terrace.

The immediate cause of the present restoration arose from an accidental flood. In stripping back damaged plaster in the large drawing room a trussed partition was revealed which proved that an unsightly RSJ inserted across Adam's Dining Room apse below, was an unnecessary intrusion. The removal of this ugly beam produced an aesthetic improvement out of all proportion to the modest structural work involved and this was to be characteristic of much of the programme of repair.

The primary documents are the Adam Office Drawings preserved in the Soane Museum in London. The history of the patron and his house was summarised by James Boswell with commendable succinctness:

> this respectable English judge who will long be remembered in Scotland where he built an elegant house and lived in it magnificently.

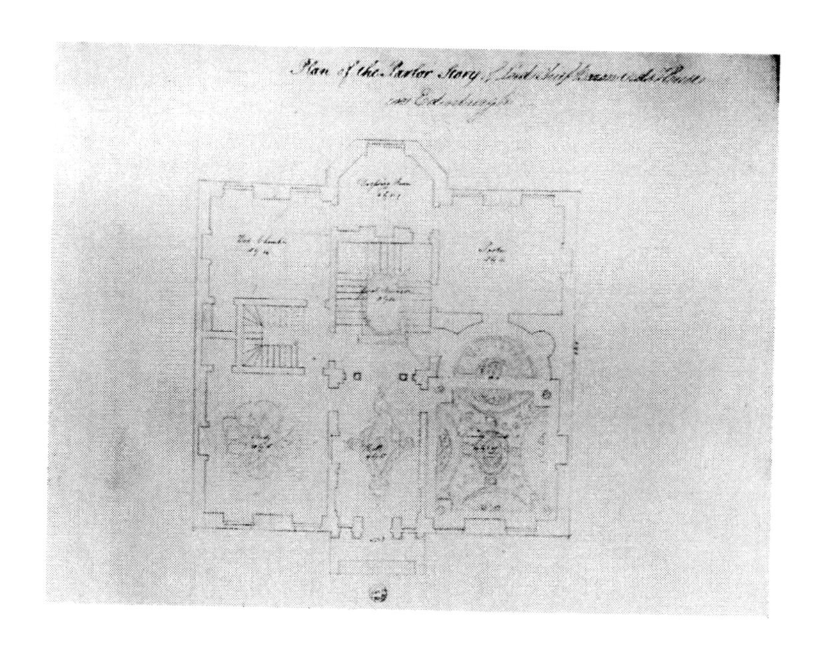

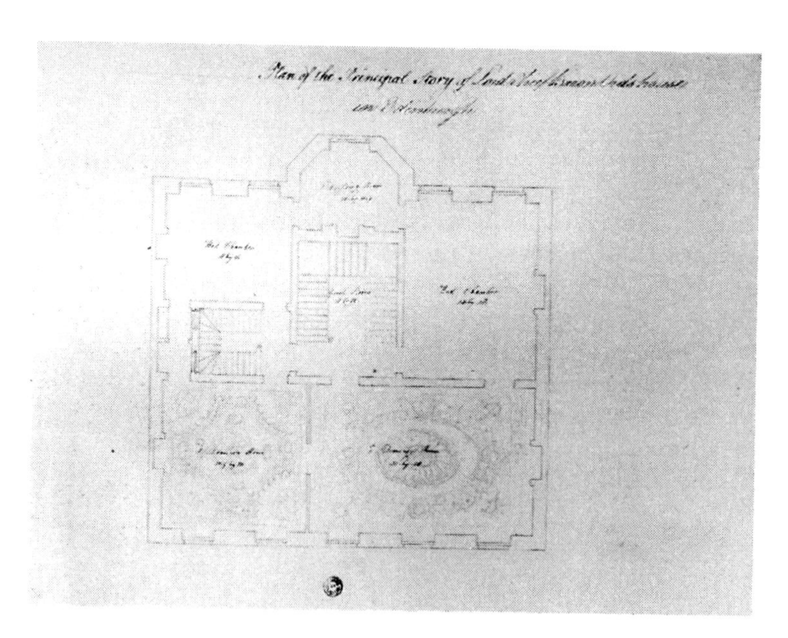

6.2. Robert Adam. Plans of the Principal and Parlour Storeys of 8 Queen Street, 1770-71. The plans were reversed, left to right, when the house was built. (Reproduced by permission of Soane Museum)

Although a great deal is now known about the career of Baron Ord and the reason for his translation from England to Edinburgh as a result of the researches of Dr. Andrew Doig, a fellow of the College, and Margaret Swain, the construction of his splendid house is sadly undocumented. With its five bays the house is conceived on a grand scale but its original extent was enhanced not only by a tunnel from the area extending under the road to a large private garden now absorbed into Queen Street Gardens but also by a range of offices rising Southwards up the hillside towards Thistle Street (Figure 6.1). For an as yet unknown reason the house was built in mirror reverse of Adam's surviving office design (Figure 6.2). The drawings confirm that Adam's two Drawing Room ceilings were executed and that the chimneypieces subsequently reset in the Hall and Study had been the original chimneypieces of the Large and Small Drawing Rooms respectively. This must have been the result of alterations made to the Drawing Rooms c. 1820 when Adam's single connecting door was replaced by large folding double-doors and a pair of austere Greek Revival chimneypieces were inserted. The double doors followed faithfully the design of Adam's original doorheads which were reset in the First Floor Bedroom, now the Third Drawing Room in a circuit of reception rooms which sought to emulate the First Floor parade suites which were characteristic of Moray Place, the most fashionable residential street during the 1820s.

The College's policy was to make the most of the surviving decorative features but the archaeology revealed by the building always took precedence over Adam's surviving designs which had not been fully realised. Plans proceeded on the basis of an experimental fully furnished model with suggested colour schemes prepared by Simon Montgomerie, the well known Scottish model maker, and Ian Gow, an authority on historic Scottish Decoration, who acted as consultant on the interior finishes.

The removal of the lift shaft totally transformed the house in a way that was fully commensurate with the decibels that were created as it was wrenched from the very bowels of the house. With the principal disfigurement removed, it was possible to refine the strategy for restoration. The importance of recovering the original design required the reinstatement of Adam's Drawing Room chimneypieces and this was achieved successfully by the late Jack Howells. Surprisingly, it was discovered that due to a miscalculation of the lintels which were rather too low, the plinths of the chimneypieces had to be cut down. The plinths were reinstated to the square blocks intended by Adam. A new hot water heating system in old-fashioned low coiled radiators enabled the window reveals to be unblocked recreating Adam's volumes. The large double doors between the Drawing Rooms, as useful now as when first installed for large parties, had to remain.

Meanwhile work proceeded with the investigation of Adam's ceiling colours through sectional analysis carried out by Rab Snowden and John Currie of Historic Scotland's Stenhouse Conservation Centre. This work also confirmed the suspicion that much of the woodwork and plasterwork of the Large Drawing Room was modern. As seems to be frequently the case in Adam restoration schemes the suggested colours given in his drawings bore little relation to the actual colours discovered on the ceilings. The Large

Drawing Room, rather disturbingly at first, had a simple scheme in which the white ornaments were set against backgrounds of identical blue which varied in strength from panel to panel and was immediately reminiscent of Wedgwood jasper ware. In the Little Drawing Room a subtle scheme of green, French grey and lilac had been the reality rather than the contrasted pink and green suggested on Adam's drawing.

In the redecoration the character of the house was an important consideration. No. 8 is of great interest in that, in spite of elements of fashionable metropolitan detail, the execution of the house follows rather more old fashioned Scottish idioms. It was therefore felt that the temptation to over-dress the rooms must be resisted to preserve their simple handsome forms. The modern schemes had also to be practical for the College's modern purposes and could not be purely academic in nature.

The ceiling colours revealed by the sections were matched in flat oil paint with the white ornaments set against coloured grounds. All the other woodwork was finished in white, including the dados, although Adam had certainly used coloured dados and skirtings in his southern work. There was some evidence to suggest that the wallfaces had originally been papered and a fine trompe l'oeil paper of interwoven ribbons of c. 1840 survived on the pier of the Large Drawing Room. It was therefore decided to finish the walls in colours which toned with the principal ceiling colours which allows for wallpaper at a later date when knowledge of what has been used in Edinburgh at this date, and the technology of reproduction, improves. It would probably have been the colours of the original textiles and papers which suggested harmonising ceiling colours as Adam himself described in his discussion of his designs for Kenwood. The reinstatement of a Neo-Classical colour balance transformed the rooms into more coherent architectural statements than Kininmonth's scheme with its lustrous orange paper used in both Drawing Rooms. The two Drawing Rooms now have distinctive, yet harmonising schemes realising Adam's ideas of contrast and movement. This new sense of architectural effect was further promoted by the reinstatement of the original heavy glazing bars whose section is properly described by their standard Scottish nomenclature as 'astragals'.

Although Whytock and Reid's pair of gold trellis pattern carpets woven in 1955 have had to remain, at least in the short term, an eighteenth century feel was imparted to the rooms by the re-statement of simple, unfussy pull-up curtains made by Ann Lister. The height of their pulley-boards was established archaeologically by feeling for their original dooks. In keeping with then current practice, the colours were matched to the walls. To contain costs, mercerised cotton was substituted for the original silk. Unlike most reproduction pull-up curtains which are too blousy, the width was merely one and a half times that of the window which appears to be the correct formula. They are pulled up tight against the pulley-boards during the day, clearing the architraves, whereas modern taste favours a more slovenly half-mast.

The College is the fortunate possessor of a fine run of medical portraits and those most appropriate to a late eighteenth century house were transferred to No. 8. By modern

6.3. The Drawing Rooms at 8 Queen Street, after restoration. (Photos Simpson & Brown, Architects)

standards they are hung high. Lighting historic rooms is a difficult problem but picture lights appeared to offer a solution. Although the College also possesses a fine collection of antique furniture, some with an excellent New Town provenance having been made for their original George Street Hall, there was nothing of an appropriate Drawing Room character. To recreate an architectural effect, as also to fit them for modern receptions, it was desirable to restore the pier tables and glasses which must have lined the window walls originally. Andrew Johnstone of Simpson and Brown designed both tables and glasses on the basis of models published by Eileen Harris in her *The Furniture of Robert Adam* (1963). The prototype for the glasses was suggested by the Chippendale pier glasses in the Drawing Room at Paxton. These appeared to have the merit of simplicity but in practice the Queen Street piers are irregular which demanded careful measurement and adjustment to the designs. Their ornaments came from Jackson's catalogue. Semi-circular pier tables seemed most appropriate for accommodating large parties in comfort and the sunk die in their painted marble tops was copied from the Adam chimney-shelves in these rooms, creating a unity of effect in the spirit of Adam himself. There was no attempt at pastiche and the virtue of Johnstone's design for the tables (executed by Charles Taylor) is their very architectural massiveness, in line with eighteenth-century practice when such items would often have been the architects', rather than the upholsterer's, responsibility. In a final refinement the simple cloak-pins which restrain the curtain cords are also architect designed and understated.

The chairs in these rooms are the result of Margaret Swain's researches. She had long been fascinated by the presence among Adam's Soane Drawings of elaborate designs for Neo-Classical embroidered chair covers for Baron Ord. It was apparent that their precise dimensions must have arisen from a requirement to fit existing frames and it may be that Baron Ord transferred to Queen Street furniture originally supplied for Dean House where he had first set up home in Edinburgh. The design of the ornaments on the chair seats followed those on the ceiling of the Large Drawing Room. It was not possible to replicate the embroidery but chair frames were made up by Trist and McBain to Adam's dimensions to allow for this possibility in the future. The frames were based on a simple standard Chippendale pattern. They were upholstered by Priscilla Williamson who went to considerable pains to find striped linen for their case covers to match the prevailing blue and green of the two Drawing Rooms. Although there had been some initial unhappiness with the height of pictures, once the ensemble was complete, the overall effect was convincing (Figure 6.3).

The adjoining bedroom was given a simple fire-surround in an Adam idiom and painted in a similar way. Because this room has to serve as an occasional Dining Room, the adjoining bay-windowed dressing room had to be fitted as a modern kitchen. The small Western Bedroom now serves as a link to No. 9 Queen Street and its pink scheme was suggested by traces of colour now found on its walls. A remarkable ghost of an oval glass was found on the pier and left for inspection behind a picture.

To play up the colourful Drawing Rooms, the entrance Vestibule and stair were soberly treated, creating an almost exterior hardness, in line with eighteenth-century practice, with a stone colour on the walls. The Vestibule was given a new stone chimneypiece to replace that transferred to the Drawing Room and the pavement both here and in the stairwell was carefully repaired. A new draught screen with an inner glass door was created by pulling forward the consoled doorcase to the main door because No. 8 was now intended as the principal entrance to the College.

Although the Ground Floor rooms retained their original forms, they had lost their Adam ceilings, although it is possible that the full decorative scheme had never been completed. It was decided to install them and this ambitious project depended on the skills developed by Dick Reid, the York-based carver, who had earlier been involved in the repair of William Adam's spirited stucco ceilings at Chatelherault in the park of Hamilton Palace. In modelling the ceilings from Adam's Soane designs, Reid was assisted by squeezes from the Drawing Room ceilings which gave guidance as to the depth of projection. Classical Plasterers of York executed the casting and installation. An interesting feature of the original Drawing Room ceilings is their rather transitional mixture of the new techniques of casting repetitive ornaments combined with some hand modelling, creating a liveliness of treatment. Initially, Adam himself had difficulty in persuading his plasterers to achieve his desired effects.

Although a deep green was found on the walls of the Dining Room, obviously there could be no archaeological evidence to guide the choice of ceiling colours which thus gave a splendid opportunity to realise the colours shown on Adam's drawing both here and on the restored ceiling of the Study. It required some persuasion by the consultant to convince the architect to approve such an undiluted depth of tone. Unfortunately, it was not realised when this was carried out that the patron's set of Adam's presentation designs for the ceilings of No. 8 survive in the British Architectural Library: Drawings Collection at the RIBA. The conviction of the new ceilings was greatly increased by inset panels of decorative painting whose iconography reflects the occupation of the College's members. Dick Reid also carved a chimneypiece from Adam's Soane design for that originally in the room, but which had been replaced by a plain Greek Revival design of c. 1820. In view of the importance of the apse, the first of many in Edinburgh, a semi-circular sideboard based on Adam's design for that at Saltram was designed by Andrew Johnstone and made by Charles Taylor. Like the Drawing Room pier tables it was enlivened with painted ornament in lieu of carving. To give an eighteenth century feel to the room simple bordered Turkey pattern carpeting, the convention for Dining Rooms, was introduced both here and in the adjoining rooms but leaving a broad surround of boards exposed. The Dining Room has silk curtains because in this second phase of the scheme the cotton curtains had been found to not work as well as sleeker silk. It was a particular pleasure to be able to hang a portrait of Baron Ord over the new chimneypiece because this had been left to the College by his descendants.

In the study Adam's star shaped ceiling was recreated and equipped with a further circular painting by William Kay. Miraculously, Adam's bookcases built into the chimney-wall had survived intact although their glazed upper doors may be later. During restoration the doors were discovered to be of mahogany and were carefully restored. They are probably the only surviving pieces of furniture from the First New Town to survive in situ. The appearance of this room was greatly improved by the installation of modern jib doors on the wall opposite the window in place of unattractive modern doors. A particularly demanding piece of restoration was the replacement of a flight of the back stairs which had been short-sightedly removed to create cupboard space some years ago.

Curiously, in spite of the extent of works elsewhere, one of the most satisfying rooms at No. 8 is the Parlour behind the Dining Room which has survived unaltered since 1771 with its plain chimneypiece. With a new decorative scheme in an Adam idiom, it has very considerable architectural presence and its Augustan character is a result of its handsome proportions and solid joinery. It is a powerful reminder of the traditional Scottish idioms that pervade No. 8 and in which Adam's own architecture was so obviously founded.

This article is based on a paper delivered by James Simpson at the conference 'Robert Adam: the Scottish Legacy' and re-written by Ian Gow for publication.

Simpson and Brown, Architects

MARGARET H B SANDERSON

TRIVIAL PURSUIT? PORTRAIT OF THE ARTIST IN LETTERS AND DIARIES

Researchers on the Adams are very fortunate in having rich archival sources to work with This paper makes use of the substantial holdings of the Scottish Record Office to cast light on the life and character of Robert Adam and his family.

5.1. 'The truth is I am very promising Young Man, [allusion to William Adam's obituary] but there is much to be done to complete the prerequisites of Vitruvius': Robert Adam, c. 1756, portrait attributed to Pecheux. (Reproduced by permission of Keith Adam of Blair Adam)

No doubt it is of little consequence that Bob Adam's shirt cuffs were 1/4" wider than Jamie's or that Jamie's favourite breakfast was rolls and butter and honey - although these trivial facts are at least a reminder of the extraordinary amount of personal detail that must often be sifted through in letters in pursuit of substantial information. Of rather more significance is the fact that the energetic Robert first bought a wig, so he said, in order to save for business purposes the time taken up in having his hair dressed in the mornings, while James, according to a friend could not be got up in the mornings and then took ages to get dressed.

The value of informal sources such as letters, journals, memoirs and even personal memorandum books, in supplying factual information about the architect's work, is recognised.[1] From his earliest extant letters to the neatly-written memoranda which he kept towards the end of his life a vast amount of detailed information may be gleaned about his personal contacts, the existence of drawings which can no longer be traced, the founding and time-scale of building operations, the names of craftsmen, officials and tradesmen involved, the terms of building contracts and schedules of work and the extent of the architect's personal involvement with commissions which were not completed until after his death. However, it is with the more subtle although equally important light which they shed on the artist himself, his ideas, attitude to work, relations with others and the experiences which helped to form his outlook that this paper is concerned.

Robert's (and indeed James's) letters written from Italy are among the most enjoyable source material imaginable, if sometimes a little stilted as the writer tried to explain or argue at length points which would have been quickly transmitted in the effortless exchange of family conversation. They are laced with the Scots expressions which came most readily to his tongue, which enliven the copy-book English with the atmosphere of the society which the writer had left at home. They are also sprinkled with Biblical allusions that sprang quickly to minds that were regularly subjected to the cadences of the Scots sermon:

> You cannot imagine how puzzled I am to find a picture for my lord Hopetoun ... the price he allows is not Sufficient for a Tip Top and a Second Rate with those Qualifications he wants ... is the Divill of all to find ... Some good Pictures ... having Naked figures in them will not answer and his Lordship may well know without Nakedness no pictures can well be found. Italian painters are given to Nakedness as the sparks fly upwards. I forgot to flype this citation but if the Lord spare me till next occasion you shall have Chapter and verse.[2]

Many passages evoke the scenes of Old Edinburgh in which Robert grew up and the activities of the overflowing and hospitable Adam household, as well as the activities of the family's building empire, an environment as familiar to the young Adams as their domestic surroundings. When in May 1756 Robert received news that one of the form's storehouses (familiarly known as 'the shed') had been burnt to the ground he lamented not so much the financial loss, bad as that was, which he hoped that a good season at Fort George might remedy, but the fact that:

> That place of Amusement in our Youthful days, of our most innocent pleasures is no more, .. where I so oft have teas'd both Burt and Millar, where bruised thumbs and bleeding heads have been my utmost Joy, where were treasured up the Pigs of Holland and the Wood of Milton, all cracked and all consumed ...[3]

Small, delicate-looking children often make the most efficient bullies and Robert may have been no exception. Certainly his assertive nature seems to have been apparent in his youth, from this account.

News of a more serious fire, close enough to the family home to necessitate the removal of furniture to safety, provoked both his characteristic ability to seize an advantage and his self-confessed tendency to see the funny side of the most calamitous events once they were over.

> I am hopeful Wrights houses are also burnt as both our Houses would be great benefiters by such demolition, I imagine Johnie will endeavour to make himself master

> of all these burnt lands ... [they] will afford place for a fine open entrey to all Houses in the land from the Cowgate and might be made very grand.

He had varying amounts of sympathy for the Adams' neighbours, mainly tradespeople, who had suffered in the fire:

> I hope Elestops House over the Gate where we enter is all burnt down, and I am rejoiced to think that his stinking tofalls are brought low, a just vengeance ... I am sorry for poor Stirling, he is realy vastly unfortunate in many different ways ... If he had many fish in the mercat he would sell them ready dress'd as I suppose they would be fried with the Heat. I dare say Robert Millar wou'd have wish'd to have been beyond Berwick when this stroke of Providence humbled his fat wife and broke his Tippany Bottles . .. As to Mrs Alison, her son is a good lad and will take care of her. He is Clerk to the Chappell [the Hammermen's Incorporation] and will procure a Contribution which I hope will make her better than ever. Besides, I always thought her a Compos'd woman and one resign'd to the will of her Maker.[4]

The Adams lived between two worlds. One was that of the tradespeople and craftsmen with whose circumstances they were familiar from everyday contact, whose practical skills they relied upon for the execution of their own commissions. The distance between them and these people was measured not physically but in terms of professional training: as Robert put it at the start of his studies in Italy, the difference between William Chambers and himself was like the difference between himself and the kenspeckle Deacon Mack of the Edinburgh masons. Not quite, because he himself belonged to Chambers' world and once he had mastered its skills he fought to extend the authority of the professional architect in the decision-making that accompanied a great building project, not without opposition from the tradesmen, as we know.

The other world with which the family was in contact was the polite society of their own employers (as Robert sometimes called them) to whom they sold their professional expertise. But here, because of a shared enthusiasm for the artistic side of the architectural business, and its literature, it was possible to establish friendly relations, as William Adam and his family did. In March 1755 Robert was genuinely saddened to learn of the death of the Earl of Hopetoun's daughter, the young Lady Drumlanrig, 'who has been unlucky since her marriage ... I wonder to whom she'll leave my Box with colours which I made her a present off'.[5]

7.2. 'An opportunity that does not occur once in a century': the rejected design for the Cowgate Arch, South Bridge Scheme, 1785. (Reproduced by Permission of Soane Museum)

Personal rapport apart - or even notwithstanding - Robert as a young man was concerned that patrons should properly appreciate his skills on which they were dependent.

> I rejoice at Jamie's account of the Earl of Hopetoun's behaviour. I hope he will grow wiser as he grows older and will every day become more and more enabled to judge the Deserts of the Adam's whom he will think it his honour to carress and use as Friends and not as Scullions, which will naturally produce gratitude in us and make us esteem him as a Friend and Gentleman, not as a Boor and Nobleman.[6]

In the winter of 1756 he reported that he was 'making good useful and noble Acquaintances which sooner or later proves advantages to we aspiring and presumptious upstarts'.

The proper study, over the last two decades, of all aspects of Robert's Scottish work has brought a welcome element of continuity to our picture of his entire career, not least in the way that it has given significance to his early training and experience, to the influence of his father and his practical experience as John's junior partner before leaving home. His study-tour in Italy was seen by the family in the first instance as an opportunity to enhance the firm's already considerable reputation at home and his later settling in London as an expansion of the firm's operations - the way in which many Scottish businesses expanded. Nevertheless, these linked developments - study in Italy and setting-up in London - were for Robert an important change of direction and personal challenge.

Although when he left home in the autumn of 1754 he had expected to return, there had been some change in his aspirations before then. His statement, that 'at London I first felt the change of taste grow on me from that I had contracted in Scotland', was made in advance of the first suggestion of the London venture in April 1755. His first sight of London probably dated from a family trip there in the winter of 1749-50. This is recorded in an incomplete Journal kept by John, who was more interested in the extent to which the Northumbrians had improved (or had failed to improve) their policies than in the appearance of country houses.[7] He did record how Robert and he gazed curiously at the remains of the Roman mosaic pavement at Aldborough near Boroughbridge, and admired the drawing of a Gothic spire in their lodgings at Tweedmouth. The Journal breaks off just as the family, including Mrs. Adam and Jenny, were settling into their London lodgings. The experience was stimulating enough for Robert himself to make another trip to England later in 1750 and he stole over the Border towards Carlisle (partly perhaps for official reasons) in the summer of 1752 when John, stranded on his own at Fort George, instituted a search for him.

Once the decision to settle in London had been taken Robert realised that it would require more preparation than if he had been returning to Edinburgh and more original ideas than the

> sett of new thoughts, which with some little instruction in Drawing I imagined would be sufficient to make one who had seen so much carry all before him in a narrow countrey where the very name of a Travellour acquires respect and veneration.[8]

We believe that what Robert left behind was an honourable and outward-looking architectural tradition to which his own father had made an enormous contribution. Nevertheless, there were aspects of the professional environment that failed to satisfy him. Why? The most simplistic explanation is that he felt himself too good for Scotland. The famous remark about his genius being thrown away on Scotland, usually cited in support of this explanation, should be read in context as part of a characteristically exaggerated passage on his prospects which was aimed at enticing his sisters to come and keep house for him in London, a project by then under active discussion with his brothers. The passage began with his asking whether the family thought his last letter to Lord Hopetoun had been

> becoming the dignity of an architect who expects to dispise Inigo Jones as he did Deacon Jamieson, to regard Palladio as Deacon Butter and Chambers as an inferior genius. I often think what a pity it is that such a genius shou'd be thrown away upon Scotland where scarce will ever happen an opportunity of putting one noble thought in execution. It would be a more extensive scheme to settle a family also in

> England and let the Adams be the Sovereign Architects of the United Kingdoms, would you have any objections to a London life Nell ...?[9]

At the end of 1755 he admitted,

> To tell the truth there is nothing I shoud dread more than returning to Scotland where so much is expected and so little opportunity of ever showing away, that I should very soon be despised for one who can show anything good for a hundred pounds.[10]

What he meant by the ill-informed expectations of the Scots was clarified in a tirade which he penned in October 1756 in answer to a letter from Helen who had passed on to him a mixture of compliment and criticism from home:

> The fickleness of the Scotch and particularly of the Edinburghers is notorious to all that have eyes. No player, no singer, no preacher, no Architect, tho' a Lacey, a Storer, a Whitefield or an Adams will please them above a season. Their great heat is changed to a shivering coldness. Their furious Affection to disgust ... This opinion of the Scotch in general I have and this it was alone made me venture a new life amongst people more immersed in business where you are not exposed to such particular Censure and where everything that pleases, will please more as no such mighty matters are expected. What Honours you come to you obtain gradually and in ten years your Character becomes general and you are courted by all, whereas after 5 months ... in Scotland you are no more minded than if you had never travelled. In short, if you have only a necessary house to build they would look for a St. Peter's Church, and on finding that Commodity (which if invented by the great Architect of Heaven) woud be nothing but a simple stinking closet, they would turn on their healls [and here he puts words into the mouth of his Uncle Archibald Robertson who took a pretty dim view of Grand Tours] and like Bauldy or his friend the Doctor exclaim 'Hi, Hi, Hi, Is that all he's learn'd abroad. I think I've just seen as good ... and better too built by our Archie Handyside that ne'er was out of Fisheraw a the Days of his life ... I always told my sister and my nieces that he was but Losing his Time in Italy ...' Thus are we great people judged by the

> undistinguishing scum of people, sans gout et sans charite ....

He may be exaggerating the number of Scots who felt like Uncle Bauldy, although it suggests he had come up against a fair number of them, but this outpouring, clumsily expressed though it is in places, is quite a subtle reading of hard-headed people whose lack of discernment makes them dismissive of works of art of real merit while at the same time demanding something spectacular. A telling sentence near the end of this passage is put into the mouth of Robertson's companion:

> I think John, Mr. Adams ... does as weel to the full as Robert. For there is my Lord Milton's house, conscience, Mr. Robertson, I never saw a better thing, Sir.[11]

Does this suggest that Robert had found the house-style determined by John as head of the firm, and easily understood by the critics, a source of frustration?

When the gamble of London was on Robert was the obvious member of the family to risk it. Because of our hindsight we may be in danger of minimising what he took on. The 'extensive' London scene as he called it was a competitive field for anyone arriving as he did with a few introductions, depleted capital, financial support from a fund that was already supporting two households, his stock-in-trade in several portfolios and a travelling trunk - admittedly of 'most enormous magnitude' - his investments in a crate 'to follow', a small recently-formed band of assistants but no colleague of similar professional experience, and with even house hunting ahead of him. If we feel unhappy about the assertive side of his temperament, we should perhaps consider that to succeed in these circumstances may have needed more than genius alone for the man who, in Mordaunt Crook's memorable phrase, 'forestalled the Greek Revival'.

It is also easy to exaggerate the speed with which his London career took off. Two years is a long time in a new business if nothing much is happening and 1758-59 were fairly slow for Robert Adam. He had some bad moments while waiting for the polite remarks of those who 'went away enchanted' with his drawings to turn into orders, or social invitations to turn into requests for plans, or those clients to whom he submitted drawings to clinch the deal.

> I wrote you Laurie Dundas had got a plan for a Court of Offices from me', he wrote to James on 11 August 1758, 'which whilst I was making some corrections upon He went off to Scotland, left the Plans in my Hands without once saying a Syllable about them. Nobody thinks of paying and when they do give you nothing worth taking so may the Divill damn them

> altogether. I'll turn soapboiler and Tallow Chandler. They grow rich and eat Turtle.[12]

Later the same month when he was genuinely concerned about lack of income he wrote to James about his visit with Adam Ferguson to a country house where the owner asked him to design bridges for over the diverted streams in the grounds. 'On such pityfull Objects is my attention bent'.[13] He remembered shares he was supposed to have in the whale fishing: 'would you advise me to give them both up, I think it would be best. Perhaps they are given up already. By Jove I know nothing of the matter ...'; a characteristic attitude to his financial assets.

> As yet not one scrap from Lascelles so that I begin to suspect him. Had he been pleased he surely woud have said so sooner. I hope he'll pay me for my plan at any Rate and I may venture to say it will make as good a figure in print as Chambers does, which he did for some Gentleman and put in his Civil Architecture.

After this anxious beginning it is not surprising to find his letters of 1760 shot through with excitement as his work built up, as in those about 'the revolutions at Sir Nat's' - Kedleston - where he replaced other architects.[14] There is one thing that exceptionally gifted people have in common with the rest of us: there is usually more than one side to their characters, something which is easily lost sight of in Robert Adam's case. Frequent quotation from his Italian letters has had the effect of accentuating the self-confident, competitive, undoubtedly at times ruthless side of his nature at a time when he was out

7.3. 'The Whimsical but Magnificent Castle ... on which the Earl ... encouraged him to indulge to the utmost his romantic and fruitful genius': Culzean from the west, engraved by Byrne for 'Views in Scotland'. (Reproduced by permission of RCAHMS.)

to prove himself. It is this side that comes over in the preparation and publication of *Spalatro* by which he hoped to capture the attention of the learned and fashionable world, and in the treatment of Clerisseau who, one gathers, was supposed to have felt so honoured by the invitation to contribute that he was also expected to acquiesce in the suppression of his vital role in its compilation.[15] With the gifts of a maestro and an artist's compelling motivation of self-expression Robert had an instinct for snatching at the means to his ends, material and human. At least one draughtsman left the office complaining of being overworked but there were others who were grateful for the training they received. James has left a homely picture of Robert and his draughtsmen 'trilling Italian duets' as they worked in his rented lodgings soon after his arrival in London.

He could show a certain dismissiveness of other people's concerns, absorbed as he was in his own improvement; forgetting to congratulate John on the birth of a daughter until nearly half-way through a letter:

> ... at this distance and in the heat and throng of Virtuosi I realy have as little thought of these ceremonys as can be, and the pleasure I feel is only from thinking that it makes you happy; [16]

or throwing a wet blanket on the news of Jamie's success at 'the Speaking Club':

> I am glad of it as it gives him and all of you pleasure. For myself, being so far removed from these things I should be entirely Indifferent about the promotion, as unless one has a particular Talent for speaking, which is the consequence of much reading, much learning and great practice, In my humble Judgement he had better keep out of the Society than be a Cypher like many others when in it.[17]

Yet he contributed his share of affection and esprit de corps which so characterised the 'wonderfully loving' Adam family, as Alexander Carlyle called them. The affection tended to be tacitly conveyed rather than openly expressed in the family circle, where a certain emotional control would seem to have been inculcated however exuberant they were in less personal matters. 'You need not doubt we both felt a little at parting', Robert wrote after James left him at Lille in November 1754, 'but it is needless to think of these things, they but torment to no purpose'. In a letter of 17 November 1755, when thanking Robert for taking an interest in his future prospects, James said:

> We two have all along been very little accustomed to make acknowledgements to one another for favours received. I may say our friendship and gratitude have been

> on a Deeper ... and a better footing and I have no intention to charge our ordinary way ....[18]

So far as can be gathered Robert's philosophical and religious outlook, for one who had been well catechised and preached over in his youth, was relaxed and tolerant - too much so at times for Mrs. Adams. In jocular mood, and no doubt to tease her, he attributed the preservation of his Roman abode in a violent thunderstorm to the Catholic prayers of the faithful Clerisseau, while 'I left the Lord to the freedom of His own will abhorring compulsion'. 'Why now,' David Garrick once remarked, 'the Adams are as liberal-minded men as any in the world' except, he added, that 'all their workmen are Scotch'. In January 1756 Robert was reading David Hume's History, of which he heartily approved:

> 'That Rage of Religious folly and superstition which in all ages has been the Cruelest and most unaccountable Cause of all oppressions and slaughter, Independents, Puritans, Episcopals, Presbyterians and Catholicks, all Squabbling and Squaling in their turns like as many Bedlamites seeking whom they might devour and never wearied of Religiously Butchering one another according as that Ideal fancy of Form and Fashion was uppermost in their Minds ... To these disturbances we owe our present happy Constitution . Bless the Lord O our Souls, etc., etc..[19]

It is not surprising that he became a member of the Liberal Society, founded in London in 1785 to compensate for the lack of moral instruction, due to the decline in churchgoing and the increasing popularity of Sunday leisure pursuits. The Society held Sunday lectures on moral and philosophical subjects for Gentlemen, of whatever religious persuasion, who shared liberal principles and were, as the prospectus put it, 'attached to our religious and civil rights'. As far as his social attitudes are concerned, Robert's good conceit of himself related to his artistic gifts and professional abilities. His ideal, from remarks he made from time to time, seems to have been the learned and civilised Gentleman, be he landed or not. The gentleman-amateur architect was to be replaced by the professional gentleman-architect. He put his brothers in this class when he designated them 'Esquire' in the subscription list to Spalatro, distinguishing them from 'Mr Milne'. It is simplistic to see him, even in Italy, as a snob and social climber for the sake of it. Real snobs take the business seriously, Robert laughed at the pantomime all the time he was abroad but, opportunist that he was, he made the most of access to fashionable society where he might acquire the consequence which would make potential patrons take notice of him. It was James, the man of fashion, who on one occasion standing at a function among the Roman nobility, suddenly thought of his homely family circle and was moved to remark on the contrast. In similar circumstances Robert thought:

> It is exceeding drole to See and hear people discoursing who know Nothing of one another, and I think I have acquired a knack at the Introductory Linguo which is some advantage at present and will be useful thro' Life.[20]

Perhaps the 'suavity of manners' noted in his Obituary was first acquired for practical purposes. Charming and affectionate though he was in his intimate circle, Robert was by nature on a fairly short fuse and professional courtesy may have had to be learned. Never afraid to take opposition head-on, he nevertheless adopted the professional maxim: 'that when confidence ceases the business ought to end as quick as possible'. He could hide private difficulties behind his public image. In the 1780s when John Baxter complained that it was easy for a gentleman of Mr. Adam's means to undercut him at Cullen House, the Adams were actually doing work for Findlater for nothing in order to pay back a loan and were on the brink of bankruptcy.

I have tried to explore the relationship of John and Robert elsewhere, but our fuller understanding of it must await a proper study of John's own work.[21] Temperamentally they were very different, a fact which helped to widen the gulf between them as relations broke down under the strain of their financial troubles in the 1780s. What John could not forgive Robert for in the end was the latter's failure to admit his part in what had happened when, after surviving the Adelphi crisis the London brothers, although by then John's debtors, continued to gamble with various ill-considered business ventures.[22] John's pride took the decent form of self-respect and the conscientious discharge of his responsibilities. His ideal in later life was to live the life of a country gentleman with business interests and to see his family do well, the realisation of which was threatened by the imprudence of his brothers. Robert's ambition was to leave behind him a monument of his talents, in which he was frustrated and disappointed in the mid-1780s when the family quarrel was at its height. When his practice revived in the late 1780s and his spirits rose with it he made approaches to John, inviting him to come and see his drawings for the new college. Without first receiving an apology, however, John declined his overtures.

Although John had worried about James's lack of practical experience when he left for Italy in 1760 Robert harnessed his younger brother's enthusiasm to his own capacity for work and they rode on the crest of a wave together for almost a decade and even through the more difficult 1770s. James was happy to follow his brother's lead:

> Tell Bob that I pardon him for superior merit, I am much less ambitious than Caesar, I am contented to hold a second place.[23]

During the decline in the architectural practice in the early 1780s, while Robert turned to landscape painting, James took to living a good deal at his country house in Hertfordshire and in 1785 published a book on agricultural improvement, *Practical Essays on Agriculture*. He continued to contribute to the work of the practice but by the end of that decade, even after the surge in business in 1789 when Robert's Edinburgh office had a full workload and he was calling on the assistance in business matters of his brother-in-law John Clerk of Eldin and his nephew by marriage, Andrew Dalzel, James seems to have distanced himself; his drawing for Yester of 1789 does suggest he may have been called upon to help at that time.[24] There is no evidence that Robert and he ever quarrelled but one does have the feeling that they drifted apart to some extent. When James travelled to Scotland a few weeks after Robert's death Peggy explained to her sister Susannah Clerk,

> Willy thought John Robertson [Robert's experienced draughtsman] should travel on the coach with him to discourse upon several different articles of business which James is a stranger to as he lived so much in the country and had not an opportunity of knowing much of what was doing in the architecture side of the business.[25]

Writing to the London family days after Robert's death John Clerk apologised for forgetting to mention the share James should have in attending to the Scottish business (having first thought of William):

> With all of those here ... he is in high estimation for his Taste, knowledge and execution in Architecture ... How he has suffered such shining talents to be of late obscured is another thing ....[26]

It seems that as in the early days of his London practice so in his last years in Scotland, Robert was largely alone in realising his ideas.

Whatever criticisms were levelled at him at the time or reservations have been expressed about his character since, it is a fact that Robert kept many of his friends for life. The names of many of those who gathered round the family's supper table in the house in the Cowgate in the early 1750s flit through the later correspondence: Alexander Carlyle, who enjoyed Robert's lively comments on the House of Commons on visits to London in the early 1770s; Adam Smith, who was in the House when John's son, William, made his first speech; Adam Ferguson, William Robertson, Allan Ramsay, whom Robert visited on Ramsay's return to London in 1778, reporting to his client at Mellerstain, George Baillie,

> Mr Ramsay ... is in wonderful good spirits and is grown fatter ... though not able to bustle for want of his limbs, but his Intellects are as good and as firm as ever, which makes him a most pleasant companion ....[27]

7.4. Probably the last outdoor sketch by Robert Adam: 'Northampton Church [?st. Sepulchre's] from nature - 1791', drawn in his memorandum book on his last journey home from Scotland. (Reproduced by permission of Sir John Clerk of Penicuik)

Colonel Hugh Debbeig, whose sons Robert took to the Prince of Wales's levee in 1790, had been a close friend since he came to Scotland with the military survey in the 1750s; and John Home, who as late as 1797 sent his compliments to the remaining members of the London household, Peggy and William, saying that he never forgot them.

I would agree with Professor Rowan that there is a heroic quality about Robert Adam's last years, as he coped with a growing workload while suffering periodically from the distressing symptoms of what was probably a stomach ulcer. When he set out from Edinburgh for Culzean Castle in September 1788, with John Clerk for company, he was recovering from a bout of influenza caught on the road from London and had been anxiously awaiting a letter from home where his oldest sister Jenny was dying from some form of cancer. Perhaps the sight of the newly-installed although incomplete oval staircase at Culzean helped to cheer him up.

We know from existing drawings and the entries in the memorandum books which he carried with him in Scotland from 1789 to 1791 that a good deal of work was done in the Edinburgh office in those years latterly in the home of his widowed sister and faithful lieutenant Mrs. Mary Drysdale.[28] Into these notebooks Robert meticulously copied business papers for his own reference; the detailed building contract for Seton Castle 1789, and equally detailed schedule of work to be done at Cluny Castle, Aberdeenshire in 1790, for which the existing plans are dated 1793, and details of the transactions between his clerk of works, John Paterson, and several clients, including Lord Lauderdale, whose mansion, at Dunbar, is about to be brought to life again, and the Earl of Wemyss at Gosford.

A person's handwriting often becomes larger with age as eyesight fails but, although Robert bought himself a pair of spectacles in 1791, his handwriting got smaller and if anything neater as time went on. His last memorandum book, in addition to expenses contains his account for the use of Mrs. Drysdale's house, settled on Hogmanay 1791, about two weeks before he left for London. It also contains a sketch of the 'Church at Northampton', (Figure 7.4) probably the last thing he drew from life, done on the way home. It is a pity, in a way, that he died so suddenly in the midst of business, but given a choice he would probably have preferred to die in harness.

One historian confessed to me recently, 'Its very hard not to like him'. In the end it is the work that counts and has earned him his place in history. It was surely contemporaries' appreciation of his creative ability, their acknowledgement that he could usually deliver what he claimed to be able to do, which won the acquiescence of those architects whom he occasionally supplanted as well as the admiration, however qualified on some points, of Sir John Soane, whose reference to Robert's 'unassuming manners' must be squared with our traditional image of the sanguine, self-confident young architect at the outset of his career. A few days after the founding of the Register House in June 1774 Robert's client William Mure of Caldwell gave a dinner party at which James Boswell, who had watched the foundation ceremony, met 'Bob Adams, the Architect, who was lively enough, though vain, for which I forgave him'. Perhaps after 200 years we should do the same.

This article is based on a paper delivered by Margaret Sanderson at the conference 'Robert Adam: the Scottish Legacy'

Scottish Record Office

NOTES

This paper is based on personal letters and notebooks mainly in the Clerk of Penicuik muniments deposited in the Scottish Record Office (SRO). I am grateful to Sir John Clerk of Penicuik, Bt. for permission to quote from them.

1. Many of these sources are cited in M.H.B. Sanderson, *Robert Adam and Scotland*, 1992.

2. Clerk of Penicuik muniments (SRO): GD18/4814. Hereafter cited by number only.

3. GD18/4808

4. GD18/4775

5. GD18/4805

6. GD18/4775

7. Blair Adam muniments: Section 4/225

8. GD18/4777

9. GD18/4779

10. GD18/4794

11. GD18/4823

12. GD18/4850

13. GD18/4851

14. GD18/4866

15. Iain Gordon Brown, *Monumental Reputation, Robert Adam and the Emperor's Palace*, National Library of Scotland, 1992.

16. GD18/4774

17. GD18/4793

18. GD18/4757

19. GD18/4798

20. GD18//4824

21. Discussed in Sanderson,*op. cit.*, pp. 16, 20-1, 34-6, 43, 49-52, 65-6, 68, 70-1, 78-9, 99-103, 106-7, 111-12, 118-19.

22. For a discussion of the Adams' work and business activities in this period, see Alistair Rowan, 'After the Adelphi: Forgotten Years in the Adam Brothers' Practice', *Society of Arts Journal*, vol. CXXII, September 1974, pp. 659-710.

23. GD18/4884

24. Original drawing for Yester, attributed to James Adam, is in the Collection of the National Monuments Record of Scotland.

25. GD18/4961/40

26. GD18/4974/1

27. Letter from Robert Adam to George Baillie of Jerviswood, 13 January 1778 (Original in the Haddington muniments).

28. Robert Adam's notebooks, GD18/4965 and 4968. The substance of the latter is analysed in M.H.B. Sanderson 'Robert Adam's Last Visit to Scotland, 1791', in *Architectural History, Journal of the Society of Architectural Historians of Great Britain*, vol. 25, 1982, pp. 33-46.

IAIN GORDON BROWN

ARCHITECTS OR GENTLEMEN? ADAM HERALDRY AND ITS IMPLICATIONS

The investigation of the seals used by the Adam brothers, and by Robert in particular, is continued, and here extended to encompass a survey of the armorial bearings of the Adam family in relation to the image of themselves that they wanted to convey, whether as professional architects, gentlemanly amateurs, or just as armigerous gentlemen.

In an article published in the first volume of *Architectural Heritage*, I discussed the image of himself which William Adam attempted to convey, most notably by his gathering together of engraved plates illustrating his work in a collection which came to bear the somewhat ambitious title of *Vitruvius Scoticus*. More particularly, I examined William Adam's use of a seal bearing the head of Inigo Jones; and I discussed the adoption by John, Robert and James Adam of other seals with architectural symbolism which, by their allusions to Palladio, attempted to make significant statements about the Adams' claim to architectural pre-eminence.[1]

Since my earlier publication, various discoveries and observations have been made which allow the theme of Adam image-making and self-publicity to be developed yet further. James Adam's ring, set with the intaglio head of Palladio, has been found at Penicuik House where it had lain unrecognised since perhaps the 1820s; this is the actual seal from which known impressions on James's letters are derived.[2] Moreover, it has become clear that very interesting statements were made by the Adam brothers by means of other allusive seals, crests, emblems, and coats of arms, and that therefore these may profitably be investigated. The most intriguing of all the seals will form the subject of a detailed note elsewhere.[3] The purpose of the present article, however, is to expand my earlier brief account of the Adam brothers' use of their seals and to look at the way this relates to the remarkable armorial bearings which the family began to use in unusual circumstances from the 1750s. By such artifice, and by the employment of heraldic or pseudo-heraldic symbolism in forms ranging from seals to book-plates, the *Adelphoi* subtly sought to advertise their profession as architects, yet at the same time to mask behind the trappings of gentility the suggestion of their participation in anything resembling mere vulgar trade.

John, Robert and James Adam all, at various times in the 1750s, used as a seal the image of a Corinthian column capital overgrown with acanthus fronds, and this device was employed in variant forms either with or without the motto *Divina Palladis Arte*. As I have shown,[4] this emblem was derived from the uppermost element of the ornamental cartouche surrounding the portrait of Palladio, drawn by William Kent and engraved by Vertue, which forms part of the decorative headpiece to the address to the reader in Lord Burlington's edition of Palladio's drawings of the Roman baths, the *Fabbriche Antiche* of 1730. A similarly used capital (though not the actual prototype taken as the model for the Adam seal) crowns the portrait of Palladio (also by Kent) which appears as frontispiece to Isaac Ware's edition of *The First Book of Palladio's Architecture* (1742). It is clear that the representation of a Corinthian capital was associated with the accepted mid-eighteenth-century image of the master; and that therefore anyone who himself used a similar capital as his own device was making a statement to the effect that affinity or artistic kinship with the great man was to be understood an inheritance to which the motto assumed by the Adams laid further claim. There can be little doubt that by their adoption of the capital emblem the Adam brothers also meant to suggest that they were to their profession as the capital was to the column: they were the *capites* or heads (Figure 8.1).

8.1. Corinthian capital seal, without inscription, as used by Robert Adam, 1754.
(Reproduced by permission of Sir John Clerk of Penicuik, B)

Robert Adam used the capital seal, symbolic at once of Palladio-worship and of Adam self-confidence, on a particular letter of 11 August 1754.[5] This letter is our next point of interest in this investigation, for it was here that he alluded to another seal which he was even then having designed. 'Be so good as to tell the Bankier [?perhaps young William Adam]', Robert wrote to his mother, 'to call on Peter Robertson & tell him that if he thinks the sketch of the Arms handsome that Norie is making, that he may order a seal to be cutt directly as we will not have time to await my approbation.' The reason for haste was that Robert was expecting soon to leave Scotland to join the Hon. Charles Hope on the Continent at the start of his Grand Tour. The timing of this decision to invest in an 'armorial' seal is significant. Adam was about to travel abroad in company with an Earl's brother. Appearances had to be kept up or, more accurately, invented in the first place. It would not be long before Robert became adept at claiming to belong on both paternal and maternal sides to two of the 'ancientest' families in Scotland,[6] a stratagem which he found stood him in good stead in fashionable circles in Italy.

Himself concerned for social standing, he supplied what his new companions sought to find in him as a *'gentilhome anglois'*.[7] Writing home to kith and kin he might speak of the Adams as 'we aspiring and presumptious upstarts'; but he yet recognised that 'a good lie well timed sometimes does ell', nd to the supposition of ancient lineage, and the fact of ownership of a landed estate joined to the wealth that came from industrial enterprise matched by the profits of professional activity, was added the instant gentility conveyed by the idea of armorial bearings.

Robert's letter to his mother, already quoted, bore the Corinthian capital seal in the form without inscription. The new 'armorial' seal survives first on his letter to Mrs. Adam from Paris, 12 November 1754.[9] Significantly, perhaps, it is in this very letter that Robert used a telling sentence: 'If I coud play Lords it woud be of infinite service to me.' The seal impression is only some 23 mm x 18 mm, but this and other

8.2. Robert Adam's 'armorial' seal, as used between 1754 and 1756. (Reproduced by permission of Sir John Clerk of Penicuik, Bt.)

impressions are sufficiently intact or clear enough for most of the detail to be made out (Figure 8.2). What we are dealing with here is not strictly speaking an heraldic seal, but rather one concocted to look like a proper achievement of arms, however bizarre. Robert was after the *effect* of a coat, and one which would allude subtly to his calling, as if he were a gentleman who just happened to be an architect sprung from a line of gentlemen-architects.

We may attempt to describe the seal impression in approximately heraldic terms, though without adhering to the precise conventions of blazoning. On a field represented as green (*'vert'*) by means of the diagonal lines customarily used in monochrome illustration of shields are three charges: a Corinthian column with capital and base in pale; and two objects in fess which are exceedingly puzzling. Visible in the enlarged photograph is an object in the dexter chief point of the shield which seems to be a star or a comet 'streaming proper'.[10] For crest there is a Roman pyramid: the representation of stonework is clear on some impressions. The motto below the shield is *Qui vitam excoluere per artes* which comes from Virgil, *Aeneid*, VI, 663, and may be rendered as 'those who had given life an added graciousness by inventions of skill.'

What are the two objects in fess? At first sight they might be said to look like lymphads (i.e. Highland galleys); or else they appear to resemble hanging baskets or the baskets of scales. However the mistake is to consider them too closely as if they were proper heraldic charges. They are not. Close examination shows that they are not boats; and there is no reason why Robert should have wanted lymphads on his 'shield'. If they are the baskets of scales, where is the balance arm connecting them? An identification as scales might lead to the supposition that Robert was attempting to suggest that he was endowed with qualities of balance and judgement which undoubtedly he believed in no small measure that he possessed or that in architectural taste and style he aimed at the golden mean. But they are not scales. Are they then, perhaps, the baskets in which building materials might be hauled up? That would smack too much of manual labour or the 'mechanick' parts of the building trade for the elegant young Mr Adam; and besides the 'ropes' and the 'baskets' do not really relate one to the other, and whereas the 'ropes' appear to be reticulated the 'baskets' appear solid and of a different composition. Is it possible that these 'nets' and 'baskets' are in fact intended to be rays of light falling upon clouds? But no 'all-seeing eye' or like source of such radiance is shown on the seal.

I believe that these objects are in fact representations of primitive huts. In their tent-like appearance they closely resemble Vitruvius's description of Phrygian huts, cited by him as then still-surviving examples of the simplest form of domestic construction.[11] In the form shown on Adam's seal these primitive huts are derived from the illustration published by Claude Perrault in his edition of Vitruvius which appeared in 1673. Perrault had shown such a hut with one half cut away to illustrate both its internal and external appearance, and his plate demonstrated how it was built upon a natural mound.[12] All this detail is exactly copied on Adam's seal, where the two halves of the construction are distinguished and the solid mound indicated, even down to its entrance passage which is precisely shown on the tiny intaglio.

What is the meaning of all this, and can it be related to any discoverable heraldic history of the Adam family? The second part of this question is rather easier to answer than the first, and this will be done presently. A pyramid is a fair enough crest for an architect, and this one is of a classical rather than an Egyptian form, resembling the pyramid of Cestius at Rome. It is possible that the pyramid's triangular profile may have referred to the triumvirate of John, Robert and James who had worked together before Robert went to Italy, and in whose names accounts were submitted and receipted during this period. Equally, the four faces of a pyramid may have symbolised the four Adam sons. The architectural significance of the column is obvious; and although this device is certainly not without parallels in masonic usage, it does not seem that it or any other of the charges on the seal are intended as 'outward and visible signs' of freemasonry, and, besides, Robert had specifically referred to 'the sketch of the Arms' which suggests that something of a would-be heraldic nature rather than of a masonic character was intended.

The shooting star or comet, a device more to be associated with European heraldry, may have some self-congratulatory message intended as an allusion to Adam's brilliance. By his chosen motto Robert was making a clear statement to the effect that he was to be regarded as one of those who civilised or ennobled life by the skill and graciousness of his art.

All in all, despite its superficial resemblance to a coat of arms, the seal is a bogus concoction which is part symbol of vanity and conceit, part pun on the Adam name as an on-going family joke, and part serious allusion to architectural progress. The juxtaposition of primitive huts and Corinthian column symbolise the idea of the development of architecture, from the rude dwellings of savages to the triumphs of classical civilisation. The origins of architecture lie in the rustic hut. The Biblical Adam was the first man (and presumably the first builder). Robert Adam saw himself as first among architects, a man with a destiny to take architecture to new heights. The star shining on the column points to that destiny and to the progress of architecture. The motto confirms Adam's opinion of himself as lineal descendant of the great architects of the past, the inheritor of a tradition which ran from remote antiquity to British neo-Palladianism.

No evidence, as far as I am aware, has come to light for John or James Adam having similar 'armorial' seals; but they, unlike Robert, had bookplates which now fall to be discussed. Robert used his new 'armorial' seal systematically on his letters from Italy until February 1756. Thereafter he employed a variety of seals ranging from a strangely grinning half-length man (what in the eighteenth century might have been called a 'drollery') to classical heads of different types. At about this time his brothers must have adopted their bookplates (Figures 8.3 and 8.4). These are superb examples of rococo engraving of very high quality. Their symbolism and equally their inscriptions are arresting. They give every impression of being a cross between the coat of arms of a gentleman and the trade-card of a rather superior craftsman. Within the rococo cartouche are striking devices arranged heraldically upon a shield the tincture of which is (as in the case of Robert's seal) represented as vert: a Corinthian column, similar to that we have already noted on Robert's seal, between cross crosslets fitchy in a position relative to Robert's primitive huts. The Corinthian capital, already used as a family seal, now assumes the position and form of a heraldic crest, placed correctly upon its torse or wreath and surmounting the shield. The same motto noted on the capital seals is apparent here below the shield, albeit that this position is in accordance with the English heraldic pattern, whereas Scottish usage would have placed the motto above the crest. The implication of this may be that these fine bookplates are the work of an English engraver working in Edinburgh; or else that they were done in London, perhaps under James's direction in 1758. The immediate impression is that the Adams have become armigerous. Yet the image of gentility conveyed by the coat of arms, in all the rococo splendour of this depiction, is contradicted by the inscriptions proclaiming the owners of the bookplates to be not John and James Adam 'Esquires' (the latter's plate properly differenced from his elder brother's by the correct heraldic mark of cadency for the third son, i.e. a mullet, or star) but as 'Architects'. The paradox is of a similar

8.3.

8.4.

8.5.

8.6.

8.3. Armorial bookplate of John Adam. (Reproduced by permission of National Library of Scotland)

8.4. Armorial bookplate of James Adam. (Reproduced by permission of National Library of Scotland)

8.5. James Adam's later bookplate. (Reproduced by permission of National Library of Scotland)

8.6. John Adam's later bookplate, showing shield quartered for Adam and Robertson, with inescutcheon for Littlejohn. (Reproduced by permission of National Library of Scotland) nature to that evident in Robert's design for his seal, which shows him as an architect wanting to be regarded as a gentleman wanting to be esteemed as an architect. What is the background to these bookplates?

The fact is that in 1756 the Adams did indeed become armigers. On 28 April a coat of arms is recorded in the Public Register of All Arms and Bearings in Scotland (Vol. 1, fol. 116): 'Vert, a Corinthian Column with Capital and Base in pale, proper, betwixt two Cross Crosslets fitchée in Fess, Or'. The crest is recorded as 'the Originall of a Corinthian Capitall proper'. The motto is '*Divino* [sic] *Paladis* [sic] *Arte*'. But this coat is granted to *William* Adam of Maryburgh, Esquire; and in 1756 William Adam had been dead some eight years. The anomaly of this record was not commented upon until the time of Andrew Lawson, Lyon Clerk between 1926 and 1966, who annotated the Public Register to the effect that the coat 'must have been taken out by his son John'. This certainly appears to be the case. Anxious to assume an armigerous rank consonant with ownership of the Kinross-shire estate that his father had bought, careful to observe a commendable filial piety, and proud of the dignity of his and his brothers' profession as architects and as heirs to their father's position as 'the universal architect' of Scotland, John Adam will have applied for a *de novo* grant of arms retrospectively in his father's name. What better principal charge for his shield than a Corinthian column; and, for crest, a Corinthian capital described as the 'originall' thereof, presumably in having acanthus leaves growing up round the bell and curving back where they meet the abacus, as in the legend of the source of the order?[13] Thus the Adams' greatest claim to distinction, achieved in the realm of architecture, would be given enduring allusive commemoration in the very arms which the family would henceforth bear as they enjoyed the standing of lairds, a status that the architectural talents and worldly achievement of William Adam had procured for his descendants. A first step, preliminary to this formal gentrification and the codifying of architectural allusions in legal heraldic form, had been the use of the Corinthian capital seal. This, with its associated motto, was incorporated and solemnified in the armorial bearings of the Adams of Maryburgh as recorded in Lyon Register. And so, that which began as a somewhat presumptuous attempt to claim architectural kinship with Palladio had ended as a statement of social status guarded by the full force of the law of Scotland.

The cross crosslets fitchy of the new Adam arms are derived from the Adamson coat of about 1565 as recorded in Workman's Manuscript.[14] Armory and antiquity supplied that part of the strange Adam heraldic concoction of 1756. Architecture provided the column; but this may not be just any old Corinthian column, and it is tempting to think that in its attenuated and unfluted form the design of this charge may be derived, however remotely, from column types favoured by John Adam.[15]

The architectural allusions incorporated in the armorial bearings, together with the designation of John and James as architects, lend to these bookplates something of the character of trade-cards. John and James at home in Scotland could not pretend to be anything other than what they were and chose to be regarded as: architects. Robert, bound for the great world of the Grand Tour, tried playfully to half-conceal his true profession and to shelter behind the carnival mask and domino of the gentleman with an intense interest in archaeology and architecture. In a celebrated aside he had asked his family not to address him as 'Architect' on their letters. For Robert no similar bookplate or 'trade-card' is recorded.[16] Yet why Robert should have concocted his own peculiar and wholly unofficial version of what was so soon to become the legitimate Adam coat of arms remains a mystery. As second son he should have used the arms of his elder brother, with difference of a crescent. Why he alone abandoned the Corinthian capital device (or crest, as it legitimately became) in favour of the pyramid is also inexplicable. The Virgilian motto remained unique to Robert. But even in later life, as Member of Parliament, 'Knight of the Shire' of Kinross, and styled 'Robert Adam of Dowhill', he matriculated no arms for his personal use. Robert had been the first of the brothers to lay claim to their father's Inigo Jones signet; yet he alone of the 'promising young men' took a different course in all matters relating to self-description, and to its visible symbols in seals and shields.

The progress in the world of the Adam architectural dynasty is starkly illustrated by the profound change which overtook their arms in the mid 1760s, an heraldic reflection of social change with which Robert (so far as we know) chose not to associate himself. In 1765 Lyon Register records the grant to John Adam of arms quite different from those he and his younger brother had been pleased to bear in honour and memory of their father. The allusion to the profession of architecture suggested by columns and capitals disappears entirely, to be replaced by a shield of arms stressing ancient and distinguished lineage. The blazon now reads: 'Quarterly first and fourth Argent, a Mollet Azure pierced of the field betwixt three cross Crosslets fitchee Gules (for Adam), Second and third Gules three wolves heads erazed Argent armed and langued Azure, within a border ingrailed Or (for Robertson of Gladney)'. The pride that Robert himself had expressed in claiming descent from 'two of the ancientest families' is here given armorial expression: the Robertsons had achieved their greatest celebrity in the person of the Adam brothers' cousin William Robertson, the celebrated divine, historian and Principal of the University of Edinburgh. The crest is now the much more gentlemanly one of a cross crosslet surmounted by a sword in saltier. In place of a motto redolent of architectural ambition is *'Crux Mihi Grata Quies'* (the Cross is my pleasing rest) which suggests a life of lairdly ease after position and wealth have been won through past (and now unmentioned) professional effort.

From the heraldic point of view, this change is to be regretted. For a distinctive shield had been replaced by a quarterly coat which is much less striking and more conventional; and an unusual crest ousted by one quite remarkable.
A bookplate of James's, post-dating the grant of these altered arms, shows his differenced shield with its mullet, and surmounted by helmet and crest (Figure 8.5). Known examples of John's bookplate show the 1765 shield, without crest, but with an augmentation in the form of an 'inescutcheon of pretence' on the English pattern and not recorded in the Public Register (Figure 8.6).[17] Both John and James now prefer to distinguish themselves not as Architects but as Esquires, a change otherwise illustrated by John's more-or-less complete withdrawal from architectural practice, and by James's

somewhat dilettante pursuit of the profession in London. Robert's only recorded use of the new Adam crest - albeit in the most indirect and indistinct of ways - seems to be in a tiny detail of a plate illustrating furniture designs in the *Works in Architecture.*[18] There, within a wreath, as a finial to an elaborate clock upon a fine commode in front of an elegant pier-glass, are to be found the cross crosslet and sword of the Adams, as if representing some rather arcane hallmark of quality.

National Library of Scotland

Acknowledgements

For permission to publish photographs of seals on documents in his family muniments, and to quote from other letters, I am grateful once again to Sir John Clerk of Penicuik, Bt. My thanks are due to Major M. P. Taitt for bringing the John Adam bookplates to my attention in the first place, and for letting me examine his volume containing them. For their opinion on the charges borne on Robert Adam's seal, and for discussion of Adam heraldry in general, I am indebted to Sir Malcolm Innes of Edingight, KCVO, Lord Lyon King of Arms, to ChArles Burnett, Esq., Ross Herald, and to Mrs. C. G. W. Roads, MVO, Lyon Clerk. For assistance of various kinds I am grateful to Dr. Margaret Sanderson, Peter Vasey and Dr Donald Abbottof the Scottish Record Office, and John Morris of the National Library of Scotland.

NOTES

1. Iain Gordon Brown, 'William Adam's Seal: Palladio, Inigo Jones and the Image of Vitruvius Scoticus', *Architectural Heritage, I: William Adam*, Edinburgh University Press, Edinburgh,1990, pp. 91-103.

2. This seal, found and identified by the present writer, was first shown and described in the exhibition 'Monumental Reputation: Robert Adam and the Emperor's Palace', Edinburgh and London, 1992-93.

3. Iain Gordon Brown, 'Atavism and Ideas of Architectural Progress in Robert Adam's Vitruvian Seal', *The Georgian Group Journal*, 1994, forthcoming.

4. Brown, *op. cit.*, p. 99 with Figure 4, which illustrates the version of the capital seal bearing the motto.

5. Scottish Record Office, Clerk of Penicuik Muniments, GD18/4744, Robert Adam to Mrs. Mary Adam, 11 August 1754.

6. John Fleming, *Robert Adam and his Circle in Edinburgh and Rome*, John Murray, London, 1962, p. 1.

7. Such was the form of address that Robert preferred his family to use on their letters to him when in Italy he was not to be called 'Architect': see Fleming, *op. cit.*, p. 2.

8. Margaret H. B. Sanderson, *Robert Adam and Scotland: Portrait of an Architect*, Edinburgh, 1992, p. 6.

9. SRO, GD18/4749.

10. The nearest parallel I can find for this is illustrated in Matthew Carter, *Honor Redivivus; or An Analysis of Honor and Armory*, London, 1673, pp. 228-29.

11. Vitruvius, BkII, Cap. 1. 5.

12. Claude Perrault, *Les Dix Livres D'Architectures de Vitruve corrigez et traduits nouvellement en François avec des notes et des figures*, Paris, 1673, Plate V, fig. ii.

13. The capital is said to owe its origin to a Corinthian maid who laid a basket, covered by a tile, on the ground beside a tomb. An acanthus plant grew up and through the wickerwork, and its fronds turned over and back when they encountered the tile. This was observed by Callimachus, who accordingly designed a new form of capital based on this phenomenon. See Vitruvius, Bk IV, Cap. 1. 9-10.

14. See Alexander Nisbet, *A System of Heraldry*, new Edition, Edinburgh, 1816, p. 129, *sv* Adamson; and R. R. Stodart, *Scottish Arms: Being a Collection of Armorial Bearings, AD 1370-1678*, Edinburgh, 1881, Vol. II, p. 144.

15. Major Michael Taitt points out to me the close similarity with the attenuated and unfluted shape of the columns forming the porch of Letterfourie, Moray; but this house is, of course, much later than the date of the Adam grant of arms.

16. There is no example in the vast Stevenson bookplate collection in the National Library of Scotland, which includes specimens of the plates of John and James Adam (JAS/1 4. 4/5).

17. The coat of arms shown on this bookplate is interesting. The inescutcheon bears the arms of Littlejohn of Woodston, granted 1761 ('three arrows gules, the middlemost in pale, the other two in saltire, points downwards, banded together vert, between six trefoils slipped of the last, two in chief, and as many on the flanks and in base'). One might expect this inescutcheon, suggesting as it does an heraldic heiress, to represent John's wife; but she was Jean Ramsay, apparently no relation to Littlejohn of Woodston. In a still later version of the Adam of Blair Adam arms (matriculation of 1882), the Littlejohn coat has become the second quarter of the Adam quarterly shield. The entire Adam genealogy is silent as to any Littlejohn connection. It seems, however, that the presence of the Littlejohn coat indicates not a marriage but the acquisition by entail of the Litlejohn estate in Kincardineshire. By 1777, when he married the daughter of the

10th Earl of Elphinstone, William Adam, eldest son of John Adam, was described as 'of Woodston'. John has been served heir of tailzie to Forbes of Thornton (1769), and Forbes in turn had been heir of tailzie to Littlejohn of Woodston who had died in 1764. (I am grateful to Dr Donald Abbott for help in solving this puzzle.) That the bookplate in question is indeed that of John Adam the architect seems certain from the evidence both of a volume of drawings from Blair Adam, sold at Sotheby's in 1981 and now n the Victoria and Albert Museum, which bears this bookplate; and of a book of mathematical tables and formulae in the possession of Major Taitt, which bears at the front John Adam's first armorial bookplate ('J. A. Architect') and at the back his subsequent heraldic bookplate ('J. A. Esquire').

18. Vol. I, plate viii.

DAVID KING

IN SEARCH OF ADAM

This paper mentions some of the additions to and deletions from Robert Adam's Scottish oeuvre that were made by the author in his recent catalogue of the architect's works. In preparing that catalogue, he made a close study of the Adam drawings in Sir John Soane's Museum and the paper also mentions some interesting observations based on these drawings.

My search of Robert Adam's works began in 1970 when I was first entranced by the flair and variety of his works, but it was many years before I contemplated writing a book. It was the absence of any other *catalogue raisonné* that made a publication of my records seem a useful contribution to the 1992 bi-centenary celebrations. In recording here the additions and deletions to Adam's Scottish *oeuvre*, the most appropriate starting point is clearly the extensive list given in Howard Colvin's 1978 *A Biographical Dictionary of British Architects.*[1]

Colvin's list of Adam's Scottish works is very complete. In compiling it he was greatly helped by the National Monuments Record for Scotland who have photographs of almost all Adam's drawings for Scottish works - most of these drawings are in Sir John Soane's Museum in London - and photographs of most of Adam's executed works. My additions to Colvin's Scottish list are mostly relatively modest works where the NMRS records are less complete. These works include estate buildings and - paradoxically for a monuments record - monuments!

Robert Adam worked with his older brother John from around 1748 to 1754. This period is not covered by drawings in the Soane Museum, so it is likely that even now our knowledge of it is far from complete. The Scottish works that I would add to those in Colvin are: the stables and other offices at Banff Castle, Banff, 1750-52 (for Lord Deskford); the Argyll Arms Hotel, Inveraray, 1750-56; the west front of the mausoleum at Yester House, Gifford, 1753 (for the 4th Marquess of Tweeddale); the additions and alterations to Castle Grant, Grantown-on-Spey, 1753-60 (for Sir Ludowick Grant, Bt.); and Alva House (demolished, probably, 1822), Edinburgh, c. 1754-55 (for Sir John Erskine, later 1st Lord Alva).

From 1758 till his death in 1792, Robert Adam was based in London, though in the later years he spent much of his time in Edinburgh. From this period the following Scottish works should be added to those given by Colvin: Bellevue House (demolished c. 1845), Edinburgh, 1774-75 (for Major-General John Scott); an addition to Ardincaple Castle (demolished 1957), Helensburgh, 1774 (for Lord Frederick Campbell); the monument to the 3rd Earl of Glasgow at Kelburn Castle, Fairlie, 1775; the stables at Dalquharran Castle, Dailly, 1785-89 (for Thomas Kennedy); and the farm, viaduct, arches, stables and

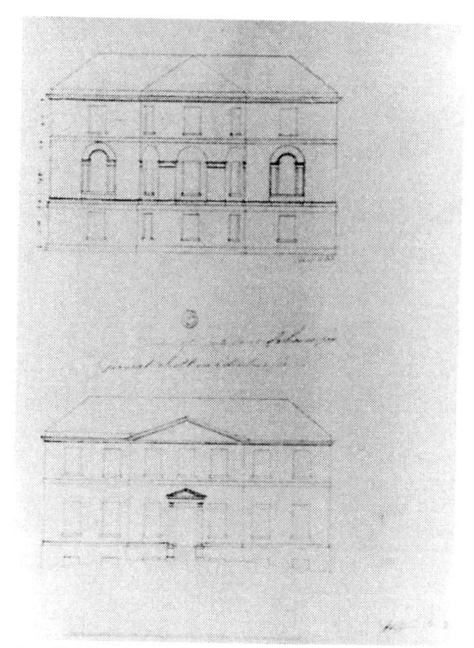

9.1. Bellevue House, north and south (entrance) elevations, 1774. (Reproduced by permission of the Soane Museum)

9.2. Monument to 3rd Earl of Glasgow, Kelburn Castle, 1775 (Photo David King)

garden walls at Culzean Castle, Maybole, 1777-90 (for the 10th Earl of Cassillis). Adam also prepared a preliminary scheme, and perhaps the simpler executed scheme, for Elderslie (demolished 1920), Renfrew, 1776 (for Alexander Speirs) and he was credited by the nineteenth century architect Walter Newall with the monument to Hugh Lawson, who died in 1781, in St. Michael's churchyard, Dumfries.

In addition, the following Scottish works shown as possibles by Colvin can now be regarded as confirmed: the Riding School (demolished c. 1828) in Nicolson Street, Edinburgh, 1763-64; the octagonal farm at Kirkdale House, Carsluith, c. 1790 (for Sir Samuel Hannay, Bt.); and the stables at Fullarton House, Troon, c. 1790 (for Colonel William Fullarton).

Only two Scottish works need deleting from Colvin's list. One is Alva House (demolished), Alva, where it is clear that the embellishments and extensions that Adam proposed in 1789 for John Johnstone were not executed. It also seems clear that Adam did not add a wing to Kilduff House, Athelstaneford, in 1770 for John Home.

Of all the additions noted, the most substantial was Bellevue House (Figure 9.1).[2] Like several Adam houses, Bellevue was given movement with a central pedimented projection on the front and with a central bowed projection on the rear. Adam's plans show an oval drawing room behind the bow. This would have been one of his very few elliptical rooms - the celebrated staircase at Culzean Castle is his only surviving example. Bellevue is best known from the 1829 view in Thomas Shepherd's *Modern Athens* which shows it in Drummond Place, but when the house was built it was surrounded by parkland. By 1829 the house had been given an extra floor which may have been added when it was converted into an Excise Office.

Perhaps the finest addition is the monument at Kelburn (Figure 9.2). This is in the form of a pyramid, on a narrow rectangular base, and it has a fine site overlooking a deep ravine. Adam's drawing records that the monument cost the client £300 - £30 for the pyramid, £240 for the carved details, and £30 for the architect who worked on '3 or 4' different ideas. The main alternative idea to the monument as executed seems to have been to give it a pentagonal base, with a shallow pointed projection at the rear, presumably for greater stability. Unfortunately the sculptor is not known, but certainly the woman who stands grieving by a funereal urn is very accomplished.

9.3. Monument to Robert Adam in Greyfriars Church, Edinburgh, designed in 1774 and shown here in the course of manufacture in 1992. (Photo David King)

There is a further Scottish monument to add to the Adam oeuvre. This is in memory of Robert Adam himself and is in Greyfriars Church, Edinburgh (Figure 9.3). It was unveiled on 13 November 1992 to commemorate the bi-centenary of Adam's death. It has always seemed unfortunate that Adam had no monument. The most obvious place would be Westminster Abbey, London, where he is buried, and following a suggestion from me, Charles McKean of the RIAS wrote to the Abbey suggesting that a monument be erected there. The response was that, owing to extreme pressure of space, the Abbey could not grant a monument to someone who also had a named slab on the floor. Happily Greyfriars Church agreed to find space for a monument and I proposed that a simple Adam design be used.[3] The design is dated 1774. The only inscription on it is 'Mrs Calderwood', written in a later hand, so it is hard to know if it was ever made for the person for whom it was originally intended. Adam's more elaborate monuments often had ideas specifically relating to the person commemorated, but this design is embellished only with an urn and inverted torches signifying death, so it could aptly be used for anyone including its designer. One other likely addition to Adam's oeuvre may also be noted. This is the ruinous folly called Caisteal Gorach (Figure 9.4) which is on a hill half a mile to the north of Tulloch Castle, Dingwall. The Soane

9.4. Caisteal Gorach, c. 1790. (Photo David King)

Museum has four different ruin designs, dated 1789 and 1790, which were prepared by Adam for Duncan Davidson who then owned the castle; the executed work does not quite correspond to any of those designs and clearly reflects a later scheme.[4] This was most probably devised by Adam but might just have been concocted by someone else after his death. The ruin comprises a round tower flanked by two walls which have both partly collapsed at the ends furthest from the tower.

Turning to deletions, there are several Scottish works that have been dubiously attributed to Adam over the years. Among these is Lasswade church for which Adam certainly prepared a design in 1791. He proposed a building with a Greek cross shape and a shallow internal central dome - essentially a Byzantine form. Adam made contact with Byzantine architecture in Italy, notably at Ravenna and Venice, as well as on his journey to Spalato. However, he was never a copyist, and his Lasswade design is embellished with a turret at the end of one arm. The executed Lasswade church, which was demolished in 1956, was a much weaker affair.[5] It had a Greek cross shape, but it was very clumsy in appearance and, instead of a turret on one arm, it had a thin spire in the centre, an idea not echoed in any of Adam's other church designs. At best it seems that Lasswade was designed by someone who was partly influenced by Adam's proposal.

Amid all the variety of Adam's work, one feature that emerges from a study of the Soane Museum drawings is that he often designed, almost simultaneously, two buildings that shared similar ideas. Thus he designed another building that hinted at the Greek cross in shape and had a central dome. This was the mausoleum (Figure 9.5) at Westerkirk designed in 1789 to cover the graves of the parents of John Johnstone of Alva House. Here the four arms are nothing more than shallow projections, but in compensation the central dome is carried into a striking external feature. The mausoleum doorway is flanked by pairs of fat Doric columns that clearly hint at the Greek Doric order, though they have necks rather than large abaci.

Another related 'pair' of Adam works are Marlborough House, Brighton, and Sunnyside House (now Liberton golf club), Edinburgh. Adam remodelled the former in 1786 for the Rt Hon. William Hamilton, and he built the latter in 1785-88 for Patrick Inglis

9.5. Johnstone mausoleum, Westerkirk, 1789. (Photo David King)

(later Sir Patrick Inglis, Bt.). Their entrance fronts were remarkably similar, with three narrow central bays and wider end bays whose ground floors had Venetian windows in relieving arches. The Edinburgh facade was given additional interest with a *porte-cochère* and ramp in front of the central bays. The Brighton facade survives reasonably well preserved, but the Edinburgh facade was lost c. 1850 when the house was much extended. Happily, its appearance can now be gauged once again from a fine model made by Simon Montgomerie in 1992 (Figure 9.6).

A study of the Soane Museum drawings also throws some additional light on Adam's genius for planning. The plans for Airthrey Castle, Stirling, which was designed c. 1791 for Robert Haldane, are well-known, and demonstrate Adam's genius in fitting rooms with interesting shapes into a house that itself had an interesting shape (Figure 9.7). But at least it might be supposed that Adam had some freedom over the selection of rooms for the principal floor, along with their relationships to each other and their sizes. However, this design was the second that Adam prepared for Haldane. In 1790 he had prepared a rejected classical scheme which was of his typical five-block arrangement - a central block flanked by two links and two pavilions. The shape of this house was in complete contrast to the castle, but the principal floor (Figure 9.8) had a virtually

9.6. Model by Simon Montgomerie of Sunnyside House, Edinburgh, 1785-88. (Photo David King)

identical disposition in terms of room types, size and relationships. Clearly each scheme was prepared in accordance with strict requirements from the client - even down to requiring a nursery, a room which no other Adam house had on its principal floor. To think that the castle was designed within such strict constraints can only enhance one's estimate of Adam's abilities.

Perhaps the most disappointing aspect of studying Adam's drawings and compiling a catalogue of executed works is finding that so many fine designs were never carried out. In Scotland, for instance, one can bemoan the fact that his fine new castles for Barnbougle, Barnton, Findlater were never built and that so little came of his splendid classical designs in Edinburgh for the Assembly Rooms, the South Bridge and Leith Street. Happily, though, there are other fine castles and classical buildings that were executed and which can still be enjoyed. But there is one class of Adam design that seems never to have been executed - the symmetrical *cottage orné*. The only rustic design that he ever seems to have carried out was for a tea pavilion at Moor Park, Hertfordshire, c. 1764-65.

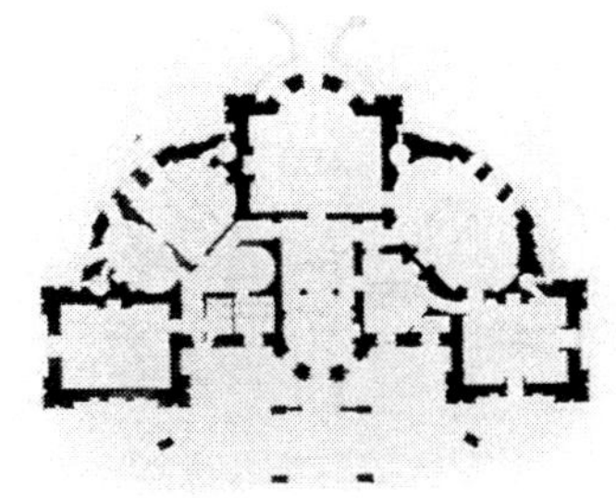

9.7. Airthrey Castle, Stirling, principal floor, c. 1791. (Reproduced by permission of Soane Museum)

9.8.Classical house proposed for Airthrey, 1790, principal floor. (Reproduced by permission of Soane Museum)

9.9. An uninscribed design for a *cottage orneé*. (Reproduced by permission of Soane Museum

Adam's *cottage orné*. designs are often uninscribed so it is hard to be sure how many were intended for Scotland, but some certainly were. One of the most striking designs is one with a thatched dome (Figure 9.9) whose drum has small arched windows recalling those on some Byzantine domes. This dome rises above a portico that has tree trunk columns and a Diocletian window in its pediment. Perhaps when the current recession is over, some modern day developer would consider building some houses based on some of Adam's cottage designs as a belated bi-centennial tribute!

This article is based on a paper delivered by David King at the conference 'Robert Adam: the Scottish Legacy'.

University of Stirling

NOTES

1. For full details of most of the additions and deletions noted in the text, see David King, *The Complete Works of Robert and James Adam*, Oxford, 1991. Since that book was written two Adam ceilings have been installed in the ground floor of 8 Queen Street, Edinburgh (See James Simpson's article in this volume); they follow the designs in the Soane Museum - volume 12, numbers 67-8 - that were made for the house by Adam but apparently not executed in his lifetime.

2. I am grateful to Ian Gow for drawing my attention to Bellevue.

3. The drawing for the monument is in the Soane Museum volume 19, number 40.

4. The Soane Museum drawings are in volume 48, numbers 103-6. One of these unexecuted designs appears in Elizabeth Beaton, *Ross and Cromarty*, RIAS, Edinburgh, 1991.

5. Attribution of executed church to Adam in Colin McWilliam, *The Buildings of Scotland: Lothian except Edinburgh*, Penguin, London, 1978.

ANDREW G FRASER AND IAN GOW

AN ACADEMIC PURSUIT

An Academic Pursuit was the title of what was certainly the smallest exhibition mounted to mark the Robert Adam bi-centenary. It has been known for some years that there are a number of cut-paper dioramas of Adam's designs for the principal facades of his Edinburgh University building, and it seemed an attractive idea to try to bring together as many as possible in a comparative exhibition.[1] Thanks to the goodwill and kindness of their various owners, no less than seven of these attractive box models were assembled in the showcase adjacent to the reception area at Old College during November 1992, together with photographs and information about another four that had been traced elsewhere. Although it had been fancifully supposed that they played some part in the design process as architectural models or were in some way connected with the necessary fund-raising, the disparity of expertise evident when the models were seen side by side in the exhibition strongly suggested an amateur exercise, more in the nature of polite handicrafts than professional model-making.

10.1. & 10.2. Pair of cut-paper models of Edinburgh University, Old College. This pair, of the highest quality, were purchased by the University in the early 1960s. (Reproduced by permission of University of Edinburgh)

The first task was to try to enumerate the surviving models. The largest group had not unnaturally been attracted by the University, though acquired haphazardly at different times and tucked away in different corners. During the early 1960s a pair of models of outstanding quality depicting the south as well as the east front had been purchased through an Edinburgh antique dealer. In fact, the distinction of this pair had not gone unnoticed during the previous thirty years, with a couple of sightings recorded by the Soane Museum in London, possessors of Adam's office drawings. Happily in 1934, when they were brought to the notice of the then Curator, Adam's biographer A.T. Bolton, he had them photographed. At a later date they were also photographed by the English National Buildings Record, and comparison revealed that both of these were identical with the University's pair. Labels on the back of the frames record that the University's set was also lent by a private collector to the Fitzwilliam Museum, Cambridge, during the 1940s. Thus, despite some initial confusion, it now appears that this is the sole matching pair: all the others that have been traced are individual models of the east facade alone.[2]

The quality of the University's master set invited unfavourable comparison with a crude version of the east front whose history previous to the University's acquisition of it in the 1970s is unknown. However, the comparative display provided by the exhibition revealed that at least some of its manifest failings were the results of an unfortunate renovation where the chosen materials of blue velvet and gilt induced a Hammer-Horror, coffin-like effect. A further model, long in the possession of the University Department of Fine Art, had suffered less drastic restoration with a new oil-painted sky but retained an elegant late-eighteenth-century box frame. In July 1955 the University Library independently purchased a further example whose rude execution was highlighted by its quite spectacular highly polished mahogany frame with an ormolu slip.

There are five more in private collections but, sadly, none with documented provenance. One is in Edinburgh, and of the three traced in England one at least was acquired in Edinburgh. The Scottish origin of one of the other English examples is shown by its original framer's label, inscribed 'Bishop, Gilder and Carver (from Edinburgh), Long Acre, Aberdeen'. It might be possible to pin down the date at which it was framed because 'Long Acre' has been cancelled and an only semi-legible name ending in 'gate' substituted.[3] There is another example in a private collection in the USA, whose possessor had contacted the Soane Museum in 1990. This is such a treasured object that the owner's first thought when a hurricane struck him home in Georgia was to pack it in an eiderdown and stow it beneath his bed.

The key model, however, because of its provenance, was presented to the Royal College of Physicians in Edinburgh during the 1930s as part of a collection of Roxburgh family memorabilia. It is also the only signed version, since the back of the frame is inscribed 'COLLEGE OF EDINBURGH by Mary Boswell now Mrs Roxburgh', and it is clear that her married name is a subsequent addition. Mary Boswell (1774-1959) belonged to a distinguished Edinburgh medical family and married in 1805.[4] She would have been in her late teens if the model was made while Adam's east facade was being erected in the early 1790s, and this gives a clue to their probable origin as a 'finishing school' exercise, which the basic similarity of the models but the very varied degrees of skill of execution would also support.

Although Adam's designs for the University were produced in the months before the foundation stone was laid in November 1789, large-scale prints of the east and south elevations were not published until the summer of 1791, to support a renewed appeal to raise funds for the project.[5] When the models were brought together it became clear that their dimensions depended exactly, to the extent of direct tracing, on these published prints.[6] Since the most elegantly executed of all the models are the University's unique pair, it seems reasonable to view these (until further discoveries are made) as the teacher's handiwork, with the pupils encouraged to try their hands at the lesser task of copying the east facade alone. The models are likely to have been made soon after publication of the prints since enthusiasm waned rapidly after Adam's death the following year, and funds dried up as attention was diverted to the Revolution now raging in France.

If the choice of subject matter was perhaps unusual in its ambition, the models fit easily into an established pattern of female enthusiasm for cut-paper work during the late eighteenth century. The most celebrated endeavour of these ladies with leisure must be the series of 'paper mosaiks', modelled from life, executed by Mrs Mary Delany, which delighted King George III and Queen Charlotte. Commenced in 1772, the series grew to comprise an entire hortus siccus and is now preserved in the British Museum. At a lesser intellectual level, many girls (and possibly a few professional craftsmen) assembled decorative patterns from rolled paper with gilt edges which were set behind glass and could be mounted by cabinetmakers to create tea-caddies, cabinets and even pier tables paying tribute to their creator's talents.

As Margaret Swain, the authority on Scottish embroidery, pointed out during the research for the exhibition, the concept of young ladies leaving their finishing schools with a framed work of skill that could be proudly displayed in the drawing room, and thus taking their place in the all-important commerce of the marriage market, was central to the success of these institutions. The fact that the poorest model of them all, in the University Library, has the grandest frame, suggesting that it was commissioned to display the handiwork of a perhaps over-indulged daughter, also fits an origin in a girls' school. Old College, as the most important public building of its day in Scotland, would not only have provided a topical subject but it may also have been fondly hoped that its choice would elevate the manual skills involved higher in the scale of the arts so that these models ranked well above the more mindless geometric patterns produced by the rolled-paper work of more typical young ladies of the period. A parallel is suggested by the frequent appearance of William Adam's engraved design for the Infirmary of 1738 on the samplers executed by earlier Georgian girls, as it was not only the most important public building of its day but also the favourite charity of fashionable Edinburgh society.

10.3.

10.4.

10.5.

10.6.

10.3. - 10.6. Cut Paper models of Edinburgh University, Old College. 10.3. & 10.6. Private Collections; 10.4. & 10.5. Edinburgh University.

In the entrance front of Edinburgh University Robert Adam realised one of the grandest set-pieces in the history of European architecture, rivalling the monuments of ancient Rome on which he had modelled his mature style during the 1750s. This set of models is a mark of the popular enthusiasm for one of the most important public works of eighteenth-century Scotland and a reminder that, far from being a spent force as English historians have tried to suggest, Robert Adam at the end of his life was recognised as our greatest architect and entrusted with projects on a scale that he had been denied in the metropolis. Since little of the structure of this vast project can have been visible when the girls laboured with their scissors and pasteboard, much of the charm of the models derives from their inevitable misinterpretations of perspectival shading on the flat elevation presented in the engraving as they struggled to turn it into three dimensions. Robert Adam would surely have been horrified by their solecisms, which embrace fish-scale rooftiles, all too prominent drain pipes and the reduction of his fastidious bands of ornament to paper fringes, but had he lived to see any of this series he would surely have been flattered and amused by this singular tribute to the high regard in which his talents were held by the schoolgirls of Edinburgh.

University of Edinburgh
National Monuments Record Scotland

ACKNOWLEDGEMENTS

Our thanks go to all of the owners, and also to others who helped in our enquiries, including Noel Anderson, Tim Clark, Richard Emerson, Joan Ferguson, Paul Grinke, John Harris, John Howard, Stuart Piggott, Margaret Richardson, Joe Rock, Alistair Rowan, Lydia Skinner, Margaret Swain and John Wilton-Ely. The exhibition itself could not have been mounted without the ready help of Martin Lowe, Iain Robb, Neil Oliver and Duncan Macmillan in the University of Edinburgh, and Roger Mercer, Graham Ritchie and Jane Thomas in the Royal Commission on the Ancient and Historical Monuments of Scotland. A collection of photographs of the models is held in the National Monuments Record Scotland.

NOTES

1. Andrew G. Fraser, *The Building of Old College: Adam, Playfair & the University of Edinburgh*, Edinburgh University Press, Edinburgh, 1989; see figs. 4.16-17 and p. 124, n. 45.

2. The University's pair of models are in identical frames and since the east facade is shorter than the south, the frame of the former is unnecessarily long. The other models are all in smaller frames made to suit the dimensions of the east facade alone, which argues against any having originally been in a set.

3. It seems unlikely that Bishop actually practised in Edinburgh as there is no entry for a Bishop in a related trade in the Edinburgh Directories between 1773 and 1825.

Unfortunately, Aberdeen Directories were not published before 1824. We are grateful to Catherine Taylor, Local Studies Collection, Aberdeen City Library, for assistance with this enquiry.

4. Mary Boswell was a grand-daughter of Dr John Boswell, who was President of the College of Physicians in 1770-72, and uncle of James Boswell the biographer. We are indebted to Miss Joan Ferguson, Librarian of the RCPE, for biographical information on the Boswell family.

5. These aquatints, engraved by F. Jukes in London, are discussed in Fraser, *op. cit.*, p. 102, and reproduced in fig. 4.7. Note that Adam's east facade, apart from the belfry, was eventually completed in the 1790s but that his projected south facade was not built; a new design was substituted by W.H. Playfair when this side was finally started in 1823.

6. Indeed in a few cases it seems that decorative details such as the coat of arms and inscription over the great entrance have been cut out and stuck on rather than drawn freehand.

SHERBAN CANTACUZINO

THE THIRD COLIN MCWILLIAM MEMORIAL LECTURE: THE NECESSITY OF ART: THE ARCHITECT AS ARTIST

Tonight I want to talk about the necessity of art, the place of art in society, the nature of art and of architecture as art, the threat to the artist and to art. To consider these things in some depth helps to understand the problems we have to face when designing new buildings, commissioning the design of new buildings, criticising the design of new buildings, preserving and restoring old buildings or just fighting for their preservation, activities, one or more of which, all of us here indulge in.

Forty-five years ago, when I first knew Colin McWilliam at Cambridge, the word 'conservation' applied to architecture did not exist. Buildings were maintained, repaired, restored and so preserved, but never conserved. New buildings in the vicinity of old buildings had to be well designed like new buildings anywhere. The idea that they were somehow a special case, which had to take into account the old buildings, did not exist. Yet the study of old buildings - the history of architecture - far from being ignored, as those who want to re-write twentieth century architectural history would have us believe, was encouraged and indeed pursued passionately by some of us. Architecture was still regarded primarily as an art, and we were there to study it with a view to becoming architects, because we had an aptitude for art in the sense that we could sketch and paint, and because we had broad artistic aspirations.

This theme is not unfamiliar to the Colin McWilliam Memorial Lectures. Last year Sir John Smith declared: 'So far as I am concerned, architecture is still an art, if even more complex than it was, and I think that the public will fare better with the artist and his outlook on the past than they will with the technocrat'.[1] And later, in objecting to old buildings increasingly being treated as documents, 'to be preserved for study, not as visual objects at all, and not for use',[2] he states: 'Architects are artists, we must cling to that. Good buildings are works of art; they are not archaeological sites ...'.[3]

For art is rooted in the realities of everyday life. Art is not possible without a patron, a client; without the principle of demand and supply, of order and response; without a dialogue. The client must have a direct involvement as the user of the building he is commissioning. It is the headmasters and teachers, doctors and nurses, office and factory managers who should be the clients rather than the impersonal and often remote committees at county hall or the regional hospital boards.

In the same way art is meaningless unless it is experienced, used, performed. Art is not finite but susceptible to change, in the sense that our perception of a particular work of art changes with time or under the influence of different interpretations. In the case of architecture, with its higher utilitarian value, the work of art itself may undergo change as a result of a change of use or a change of fashion.

This is precisely what has happened with old buildings which until recently remained neglected or despised. Didier Repellin in the First Colin McWilliam Memorial Lecture tells the story of the Singapore taxi driver who took him to the shophouse he had been restoring, asking all the way why he had taken so much trouble over a wretched old Chinese house. When they arrived, the taxi driver was so surprised to see the house looking smart and colourful, that he refused to be paid.[4] I had a similar experience on a recent visit to Adelaide in Australia, although in my case the taxi driver did not refuse to be paid. Already convinced of the benefits of architectural conservation, he told me of a restaurant - a converted old house - which its owner had demolished one night after being refused permission for an extension. 'The pile of rubble is still there,' he said with glee, 'to teach all would-be wreckers a lesson'.

'The public will fare better with the artist and his outlook on the past than they will with the technocrat.'[5] This comment by Sir John Smith places the artist in time and space. With his roots in the realities of everyday life, which are themselves part of a continuous process, the artist cannot avoid having an outlook on the past. The technocrat, on the other hand, operates on an unreal, abstract plane. 'Unlike art which is always rooted in the concrete life of society', says Dalibor Vesely, 'technique is to a great extent emancipated from the political and cultural context.'[6] Vesely goes on to explain that technique belongs to the laboratory, where nature can be systematically transformed into idealised models, and where new rules of knowledge can be developed and cultivated. These new rules are articulated in the relatively closed world of experimental dialogue, unlike the traditional knowledge of the artist which is cultivated in a dialogue with the given conditions of reality. The technocrat, therefore, has no outlook on the past, because he is concerned with the abstracted world of systems.

The artist operates in the space around him. He is space-conscious and place-conscious. He is a space-maker and a place-maker. The synthesis which the architect as artist has to achieve is a creative process which is the prerogative of the artist. The architect as designer is also the artist as creator, and this creative energy of the artist has always been associated with the search for and making of order, manifest in architecture, for example, in symmetry, balance, rhythm, the grid, the bay; the frame - what Colin Rowe, in identifying one of the major themes of twentieth century architecture, has called 'the frame as a symbol of order'.[7] The satisfying indivisible unity, which all the best architecture possesses and which is a consequence of this search for order, is a quality of art. There is indisputably a strong scientific element which goes into the making of buildings, but science and technique in architecture are essentially tools - means to an end and never in themselves ends.

'The making of order and the making of things', says Dalibor Vesely, 'belong together'.[8] The artist's search for order imitates the cosmic order and the order which is found everywhere in nature. The artist observes, interprets, transforms, reveals what God has created. He does these things in a number of ways, one of which is by the use of symbolism. Now Colin and I were brought up on Geoffrey Scott's *The Architecture of Humanism*, which puts forward the thesis of pure taste, of an architecture, as Kenneth Clarke has said, 'seeking no justification beyond that of giving pleasure.'[9] But the book which influenced my generation of architects more than any other was Rudolph

Wittkower's *Architectural Principles in the Age of Humanism.* It appeared shortly after Colin and I left Cambridge and overturned Scott's thesis. In reviewing this book in the *Architectural Review* at the time, Kenneth Clarke wrote as follows: 'The first result of Professor Wittkower's studies is to dispose, once and for all, of the hedonist, or purely aesthetic, theory of Renaissance architecture. Whatever may be the effect of Renaissance buildings on us, the intention of the architect was entirely different. Both Alberti and Palladio have left us descriptions of ideal churches. They show the lofty symbolism underlying all those characteristics which a recent generation of critics believed to have a purely aesthetic intention. When Alberti recommends that churches should be white, it was not on the grounds of taste, but because purity and simplicity of colour, as of life, is most pleasing to God'.[10]

Beauty for Alberti is an expression of these sentiments, 'something which is proper and innate, and different throughout the whole, whilst ornament is something added and fastened on ...'.[11] Clarke compares Alberti's distinction between beauty and ornament with Coleridge's distinction between the imagination and the fancy. Similarly Henry Wootton's 'firmness, commodity and delight' may result in beautiful architecture, with beauty diffused throughout all the three qualities. Wootton's 'del'ght' is therefore not beauty, but is equivalent to Alberti's 'ornament' or Coleridge's 'fancy'. Beauty and imagination, however, are not quite the same thing and it would be useful to make the distinction. Imagination may be considered as the process - the artist's imagination as the means of achieving something beautiful. Beauty, on the other hand, is the product or the successful result of the creative process. 'Beauty,' says Lethaby 'is the "substance" of things hoped for.'[12]

Alberti's imagination, like Palladio's, was fired by the architecture of antiquity, the ruins of which he could see and study all around him. But when Alberti and Palladio built, they did not copy antique models. They did not construct replicas of Greek and Roman buildings. They reinterpreted and transformed classical architecture, making out of it something new, which belonged to its time and which was at once universal and personal to the artist.

The artist's imagination is fed both on the real and on the mythical world. Nature, the human body, buildings of the past are all part of the real world and a legitimate source of inspiration. What matters is the depth at which the imagination operates. There is the superficial level, as Charles Correa has suggested, at which forms are merely transferred from one building to another. This is what most of today's eclectic architecture seems to be about. Or there is a much deeper level of compulsive imagery, to which perhaps only a few architects have access, where forms are reinterpreted and transformed into something quite new.[13] Both Correa and Richard MacCormac give Frank Lloyd Wright's early Chicago period as an example of 'a new sense of architecture within the recognisable dress of American suburbia',[14] or, by analogy, 'a language with sufficient conventional usage to make the new syntax accessible',[15] which finally succeeds in reinterpreting the aspirations of the people for whom it is built.

'All architecture', said Ruskin, 'proposes an effect on the human mind, not merely a service to the human frame'.[16] It is precisely this spiritual quality of architecture, without which architecture is nothing, that I have been trying to emphasise: the need to get back to unfashionable fundamentals and answer questions such as 'does it form an artistic whole?', 'does it have symbolic content and is it satisfying to the mind and to the senses?', 'is it beautiful?'. I now want to say something about the place of art in society and the role of the critic.

As a critic I think of myself as an interpreter of the building or work of art, and I like to recall Matthew Arnold's definition of criticism as 'a disinterested endeavour to learn and propagate the best that is known and thought in the world.'[17] A disinterested endeavour means that the critic must never write about himself through another person's work. The critic's personal opinion is not required. It is the work criticised that matters. 'Criticism,' said Sainte Beuve, 's the pleasure of getting to know minds, not of correcting them; it is an eyeglass, not a cane.'[18] Or, paraphrasing T.S. Eliot, 'Honest criticism and sensitive appreciation is directed not upon the architect, but upon the architecture.'[19] Eliot takes the creative process into consideration. Again paraphrasing (Eliot is writing about poets and poetry): 'If architecture is a form of "communication", yet that which is to be communicated is the architecture itself, and only incidentally the experience and the thought which have gone into it.'[20] For an architectural critic, the experience and the thought which have gone into an architect's work are a vital tool. The architect himself is a better architect if he is a critic of his own work, if he exercises his critical faculties by selecting and rejecting during the creative process. A critic must have an understanding of this creative process if he is to provide a valid interpretation of the end product. He must have what Eliot calls 'a highly developed sense of fact.'[21] In other words he must have full and profound knowledge before he can begin to be critical.

And this is where the creative process begins. Having marshalled his facts (like the architect), the critic has to give these some sort of order, some sort of pattern. This is a matter of selecting and rejecting, of establishing a hierarchy, of constructing.

The architect, at some stage, will allow an idea to emerge - intuitive, no doubt - to which he will cling, perhaps adapt, but which he will never compromise. Throughout the working-up of his design, he will apply the practical requirements of his brief, again and again, to this idea.

The critic's test must be to apply his interpretation, again and again, to the original - to work he is criticising. 'When has there been a piece of criticism concerned, intensely concerned, with the work itself?'[22] Flaubert's rhetorical cry was directed at literary criticism. We might equally well say the same of architectural criticism today. We might even paraphrase Flaubert loosely and ask: 'How often are architects concerned, intensely concerned, with the work itself?'

The critic as well as the architect must have two questions constantly before him: 'What is art, what is architecture?' and 'Is this good architecture?' Both questions I have to some extent tried to answer, but the second question, 'Is this good architecture, is this beautiful?' needs some further comment. Many people would say that whether something is good architecture is a matter of opinion. 'I know what I like and my opinion is as good as another's.' To say this is to suppose that judgements about art and design are wholly subjective. This is clearly not so if we consider the matter in a little more depth. Take, for example, the Royal Fine Art Commissions. The basis of their judgements is consensus. A consensus is reached by a number of people, all of whom are highly knowledgeable and experienced. Judgements about design are undoubtedly in part subjective, but the degree of subjectivity is reduced by scholarship and experience. If a judgement has to be made about the compatibility of a building with its surroundings, it is possible to do this by considering its height, bulk, scale, proportions, rhythm and so forth, all of which can be treated quite objectively.

There is after all a wide consensus about existing buildings which are good enough to merit listings, whether old or modern. Historic Scotland and English Heritage officers, who are both knowledgeable and experienced, make qualitative judgements about old buildings when they advise on listing and the Department of the Environment often accepts this advice. So why should it not be possible to make a qualitative judgement about the design for a new building?

To attempt to answer these two questions ('What is architecture?' and 'Is this good architecture?'), and to improve the quality of the answers with each new attempt, is an essential activity of both architect and critic, an activity without which architecture must wither and die, as it did all too clearly in all those central and eastern European countries in which communist rule forbade or discouraged true criticism for the best part of fifty years; and as it threatens to do in our own over-commercialised and over-capitalised western European countries. The threat to art, then, is what I want to talk about in the concluding part of this lecture.

In a totalitarian regime education and the arts are controlled by the government, the control of education enabling the government to force state-approved attitudes towards art on as many pupils as possible. For architects, engineers and planners to be forced into vast offices to undertake the systemisation first of the town, then of the villages; to design standardised blocks of housing, offices, commercial centres and industry; and to be obliged to use prefabricated construction systems, left little to the creative spirit. There was perhaps an occasional one-off house of culture, but the very name suggests cultural activities approved by the government being put under one roof for easy comprehension and consumption, as if culture was a kind of veneer to education.

Ideology of any kind, whether communist or otherwise, is the enemy of art, for art, as Herbert Read has said, 'cannot become conceptual, an affair of symbols, an activity conducted without relation to objects. Art is always a perceptual activity, an activity of the senses in relation to plastic materials'.[23] All interference by government in the arts, even if it is well meant, is undesirable. Walter Gropius, who had his share of interference by the Nazis, was adamant that art needs no tutelage; it must be able to develop in complete freedom. 'The direction of art by public authorities, central supervisory organisations and laws are more likely to destroy creative impulses than to assist them ... Therefore, the very most that the state and public authorities can do is to concur intelligently in the initiative which comes from the artists themselves, by supporting benevolently and wholeheartedly every attempt to stimulate industry and the public, and especially exhibitions.'[24]

Since 1989 there is again the opportunity, in the formerly communist central and eastern European countries, to free the arts from government control, to rid art of ideology and to return to the traditional concern of aesthetics; to the quest for 'the beautiful'; to the notion of talent, genius, tradition and the particular formal possibilities of the various arts; and especially to the notion of the artist's imagination as the spiritual means of artistic expression. In other words it is time to consider once again the success of failure of a work of art as art and not as a social document. This was so, of course, before the communist regimes took hold in these countries. Indeed they experienced a remarkable cultural Renaissance which has been denied, despised or disgracefully falsified in the history books of subsequent communist regimes. A first step must be to reinstate this period, to study it and to learn from it. A second step must be to liberate the architect by disbanding the large government project offices and declaring that architects will in future operate freely in response to demand. This second step, in other words, must be to re-establish the traditional client-architect relationship. There is no reason why the client cannot be the state or a public authority, but they must not dictate or control, but 'concur intelligently' as Gropius said, 'in the initiative which comes from the artists themselves ...' For good art cannot come about in a vacuum, but is born of an enlightened client, generous financing and a public-minded brief. Freedom once regained is a precarious condition which is forever under threat. John Pick in *The Arts in a State* [25] has pointed out that, after the Second World War the policy for the arts of the newly created Arts Council was essentially reactive. The 1951 Festival of Britain was an example of enlightened Government patronage. Artists, poets, musicians, architects and designers contributed to each of the exhibitions' pavilions. There was no separate pavilion for 'the arts'. The catalogue makes none of the claims that it would today, for the social, educational and economic effects of the arts. They are just assumed to be worthwhile in themselves and because they add a spiritual dimension to people's lives.

Today in Britain we see this freedom eroded. The arts tend to be seen either as agents of social welfare or as economic investments. They have become services or goods and, of course, the object of government policies, just like health or housing. There are many ways in which a democratic government can exert control over the arts short of censorship. Today in architecture, government departments and their statutory undertakers and arms-length organisations have to obtain the highest offer when selling, irrespective of any social or moral obligations which may be inferred in the sale. Similarly when buying, they have to accept the lowest tender, irrespective of design quality. They have become so obsessed with economy and cost control that design-build, by means of which the successful contractor may change the architect's design in order to cut costs, has become their favourite, if not quite their only, method of proceeding.

Under pressure from both client and architect, the design-build method is adapting to restore design to its central position. Compulsory competitive tendering for architects, however, provides little room for manoeuvre. The Royal Fine Art Commission saw the government's consultation paper, *Competing for Quality*, as a threat to the quality of public architecture. 'Architecture', it declared, 'is a public art and has obligations beyond the practical requirements in a client's brief, which are not merely utilitarian but require imagination. The client who recognises this, acts as patron rather than just as user. The effects of compulsory competitive tendering will cause architects to reduce their fees as well as the time spent on design. This will limit the potential for civic gestures to be made through architecture. Good design is essentially a critical process, and the creative energy of a successful designer should not be dissipated by the management processes which compulsory competitive tendering will inevitably bring about.'[26]

The market-dominated economy of Britain reflected in the two examples I have just given, means that everything has to be paid for, that the government gives nothing away, withdraws its subsidies and rejects the paternalistic view that it has a duty to provide. The effect on architecture is that, with a few exceptions like the shining example of Hampshire County Council's Architects' Department, there is no longer any patronage, either at government or at local government level. At local government level the situation has even reached the point where the construction of a town hall like the one at Epping (the result of an architectural competition and a commendable act of patronage) became an electoral liability (because it was thought to have cost too much) rather than an object of pride. Unlike the rest of Western Europe, where major developments are commissioned by government departments and are often the subject of architectural competitions, in Britain nearly all development, large and small, is in the hands of property developers who dislike architectural competitions but who compete against one another, not for the best design, but for the best financial deal.

Britain's condition is epitomised for me in Christopher Logue's little poem: 'Last night in London Airport, I saw a wooden bin labelled "unwanted literature is to be placed herein". So I wrote a poem and popped it in.'[27] But it would be wrong of me to end on such a negative note, wrong in the sense that I would be failing Colin, who was an architect, a writer, a teacher and a very positive person. Artists are extraordinarily resilient and will survive, even thrive, in adversity. Artists have been sustained in the past by even the most oppressed societies, so that the bin can be seen as the symbol of concealment, the secret container of the persecuted artist's work waiting for better times. The Sydney Opera House is the only masterpiece I can think of which came, so to speak, out of the bin, but there must be other masterpieces which were rescued from oblivion. Even if there aren't, it is enough to know that poets and artists have always destroyed their work, so that the bin becomes the container of rejected masterpieces, a source of endless riches, a deep well of the imagination and finally a metaphor for collective wisdom and the inspiration of all art.

NOTES

1. Sir John Smith, 'How Much should we Respect the Past,' The Second Colin McWilliam Memorial Lecture, *The Age of Mackintosh, Architectural Heritage III*, Edinburgh University Press, Edinburgh, 1992, p. 93.

2. *Ibid.* p. 97.

3. *Ibid.*

4. Didier Repellin, 'The Human Heritage: A Message from the past transmitted to the Future', The First Colin McWilliam Memorial Lecture, *Scottish Architects Abroad. Architectural Heritage II*, Edinburgh University Press, Edinburgh, 1991, p. 115.

5. Sir John Smith, *op. cit.* p. 93.

6. Dalibor Vesely, 'The nature of Creativity in the Age of Production', *Scroope Four, Cambridge Architectural Journal*, p. 31.

7. Colin Rowe, 'Chicago Frame', *Architectural Review*, November 1956.

8. Dalibor Vesely, *op. cit.*, p. 32

9. Kenneth Clarke, 'Humanism and Architecture', *Architectural Review*, February 1951.

10. *Ibid.*

11. *Ibid.*

12. *A Continuing Presence.* Seven Essays taken from *Form in Civilisation*, by W.R. Lethaby. A British Thornton Norman Stevenson Memorial publication, 1982.

13. Lecture given by Charles Correa at the Royal Institute of British Architects, London, on 15 October 1991.

14. The Second Bossom Lecture, 'Tradition and Transformation' by Richard MacCormac, given at the Royal Society of Arts on 18 April 1983.

15. *Ibid.*

16. John Ruskin, *The Seven Lamps of Architecture*, London, 1849.

17. Matthew Arnold, 'Functions of Criticism at the Present Time', in *Lectures and Essays in Criticism*, vol. 3 of *The Complete Prose Works*, (ed. R.H. Super), University of Michigan Press, 1962.

18. Quoted in *Dinner at Magny's* , by Robert Baldrick, Penguin Books, 1973.

19. T.S. Eliot, 'Tradition and the Individual Talent', in *Selected Essays*, Faber, 1972

20. *Ibid.*

21. 'The Function of Criticism', in Eliot, *op. cit.*

22. Robert Baldrick, *op. cit.*

23. Herbert Read, *The Meaning of Art*, Faber 1972.

24. Walter Gropius, *The New Architecture and the Bauhaus*, Faber 1935.

25. John Pick, *The Arts in a State. A Study of Government Arts Policies from Ancient Greece to the Present*, Bristol Classical Press, 1988.

26. Royal Fine Art Commission Press release, 30 January 1992.

27. Christopher Logue, 'Ode to the Dodo' in *Mixed Rushes, Poems 1953-1978*, Cape, 1978.

RCAHMS. Inventory etc. Argyll 7, 1992. £120.00, hardback.
ISBN 0 11 494094 0

Chan fhaca mi riamh leabhar air na cuspairean seo a tha cho comasach san doigh a dh'innseas e mu dheidhean carraghan ar duthaich, agus gu sonraichte, am feadhainn ann Siorramachd Earra-Ghaidheil. 'S e deagh obair a th'ann da-riribh: ach cosda air leth (£120), agus, mar sin, chan urrainn a mhor-chuid riamh 'ga'cheannaich. Tha e sealtuinn air a h-uile clach air an do dh'obair duine - gach eaglais neo cille, taigh-mor agus togalach de gach sheorsa - ann doigh cho ealanta nach robh deanta 's an tir seo riamh agus a'toirt dhuinn beagan eolas mu dheidhinn gach aon. Tha (barrachd air a'phris) aon no dha rudan cearr leis cuideachd (mar a leanas, ann am beurla), ach 'se leabhar cho cudromach: 's fhiach suil a thoirt air - ged nach bith e ach 's an leabhar-lann.

The RCAHMS was created in 1908, to record all monuments of consequence up to the time of the union. This is the final volume in a series of seven on Argyll, and it also includes a selection of structures up to around 1850. A previous volume covers the earlier period, plus (illogically) early Christian non-ecclesiastical monuments. Similar to the more recent volumes in lay-out and in principles of inclusion/exclusion, it therefore carries all the familiar features which made these volumes the unique things they are, or rather, were, as the series is now ended.

The history of Argyll is of the greatest interest: for here was established the heartland of the embryonic nation, where St. Columba founded his mission, and where subsequently was centred the Lordship of the Isles, the last and the greatest semi-independent 'empire' to be brought under crown authority. Thereafter, Argyll - especially the area covered by this particular volume - became the heartland of the Campbells, a dynasty which was, perhaps more than any other, to achieve a long-lasting political prominence on both the national and the UK scene. Not surprisingly, therefore, within the part of the county of Argyll covered by this book, there is much of the greatest interest - Inveraray Castle, its designed landscape and town; Carnasserie; the Crinan Canal; Castle Sween ('possibly', we are reassured, 'the earliest surviving [mainland] stone castle' in the country): all major monuments of their age, the first at least of international significance, a point under-stated by the decision to limit the terms of reference to 'Britain'.

Not a book for reading from cover to cover, it is primarily a research tool. A scholarly-written introduction, followed by the inventory proper: 288 individual sites, including multiple entries, so the actual number is much greater. Monuments, early Christian to 19th century, are given a description commensurate with their complexity and (known) interest, plus generous provision of photos and the distinctive 'house-style' Commission drawings. Text follows conventional formula: a technical description preceded, sometimes, by a brief outline. The intention is to provide the reader with the raw data upon which to build, rather than to attempt the last word on any single monument - indeed, in many cases, this is the first printed word. Thus, for instance, it can now be seen that Carnasserie and the Campbell of Ardkinglas mural monument at Lochgoilhead both belong to (or perhaps in the latter case, derive from) the Court architecture tradition of east-central Scotland, exemplified by Mar's Wark.

Lindsay and Cosh's pioneering work on Inveraray is up-dated, though that book slightly haunts the Commission's treatment, neatly dealt with by cross-reference in an understandable effort to avoid unnecessary duplication. Care not to duplicate means, however, that Dugald Campbell's unexecuted splay-planned design 'in the Castle Stile' for Inveraray Castle is omitted, and drawings selected for reproduction are essentially of the executed design, with the important exception of MacGill's scheme, which probably merits closer analysis for its own sake - for example for its combination in full scale of the quadrangular tradition with that of the U-plan front, previously little more than hinted at by Holyrood - rather than being included mainly for the information it conveys regarding the old castle. Campbell's scheme also deserves greater notice, given its combination of classical and castellated features, not least because this design, or the intellectual background from which it emerged, was influential upon Robert Adam's 'castle style'/court revival work, down to and including the terminology. But where such a wealth of monuments has to be described and illustrated, space is short.

In terms of content, and of quality, the book is, characteristically, excellent; photographs as sharp as the detailed examination. The commitment of staff to informing themselves of this part of the world has been absolute. A straightforward demonstration of their thoroughness lies in the number of 'discoveries', including a previously unknown ogham inscription (at Lochgoilhead). The bulk of these monuments have never been documented sufficiently, if at all, and entries such as that for Carrick Castle, with plans and textual descriptions, are invaluable. Commission pride in the accuracy of detail drawing seems well justified, judging by the drawing of the Carnasserie chimneypiece, when comparing the real thing to MacGibbon and Ross's misleading approximation.

There are things which even those generally familiar with the district may not have known: surprises such as Barbreck's Well of 1714 with inscription in Scots, and the plan of Kilmun Old Kirk by no less a person than the 9th Earl of Argyll.

Selectivity post-1707 reminds us of the original Inventory cut-off date, that date having, absurdly, been presented as a watershed in architectural history; an inheritance frustrating to reader and to compiler alike, judging by the reference to Lorimer's Ardkinglas as being, besides Inveraray, 'the most remarkable single [domestic] building' within the area (though to my mind, Carnasserie, straitjacketed in the 'Castles and Fortifications' section, might be ascribed that honour). Thus, Ballimore and the Toward driveway bridge/grotto (both probably by David Hamilton) are omitted because they post-date the union. The increasingly tentative selection as we approach our own time leads to imbalance, e.g. by the too cursory account of the 19th century marine villas of Cowal such as those at Kilmun; and any sizeable work by an architect of the stature of Charles Wilson (who designed Benmore) really ought to have been included. Rural townships and industrial monuments are, however, well-represented.

Following long-established convention brings problems, for instance, a division to be made between 'Castles and Fortifications' on the one hand, and 'Domestic architecture ... 17th to the 19th century' on the other, thus obscuring the continuity between architecture either side of 1600.

Besides the 'problems' of period selectivity and of convention, there are other points of detail one might dispute: at Toward, for instance, I should have thought the library was part of the original scheme, and not an alteration, as stated.

The book suffers also from problems of terminology, which applies in general to the wider architectural-history world, where errors are commonplace. Almost a century after Ardkinglas was rebuilt, we need no longer describe Lorimer's work in terms of 're-interpretation of Scottish vernacular' now our terminology is formalised, for nowadays, architectural historians use the term 'vernacular' to define the most basic end of the spectrum, not the architectural mainstream. It is now clear that it was Court Architecture of the 16th-17th century which attracted 'revivalist' architects - hence their use of ashlar and pediments - and not the turf of the real 'vernacular'.

A simple, though much welcomed point is the way in which the Gaidhlig background is dealt with, although there seems no 'policy' towards the language. For instance, Airigh Mhor is given a translation, while, on the same page, Ari-yerg (sic), no less straightforward, is not translated. But we appear to be mid-way in a continuum, for this book is a world removed from the Commission's first work in the West Highlands (the Outer Isles, Skye, etc., 1928), when but for the necessary appearance of place names, the fact that the culture was a Gaidhlig one was kept 'invisible'. The authors' efforts to become immersed in the culture is possibly without precedent for non-Gael Edinburgh-based architectural historians employed by central government, and is one of the book's primary strengths, for of course knowledge of and sympathy towards the culture enables an understanding of the history which would otherwise be difficult to achieve.

The Commission has now changed its publishing policy, moving to a thematic rather than a geographical approach, and a gazetteer-type series for archaeology. With only approximately half the country covered by Inventories, counties (for the meantime) a thing of the past, and earlier volumes seriously out of date, there is something sad in all that. How welcome volumes on Perthshire, Aberdeenshire, or Angus would be, or an up-dating of Berwickshire. But with only one city and five counties completed since the War, and a current volume price of £120, arguments in favour of directional changes can be seen. This is such a worthwhile and desirable book, but predicated firmly upon institutional purchase: I doubt if many private individuals will ever own it.

Aonghus MacKechnie
Historic Scotland

Iain Gordon Brown, *Monumental Reputation: Robert Adam & the Emperor's Palace, National Library of Scotland*, Edinburgh, 1992; Margaret H. B. Sanderson, *Robert Adam and Scotland: Portrait of an Architect*, HMSO, Edinburgh, 1992; Various authors, *The Architecture of Robert Adam: Life, Death and Survival; the Works in Scotland*, Edinburgh, 1992.

The failure to mount a major, all-embracing exhibition to commemorate the bicentenary of the death of Robert Adam, led to four attempts to fill the vacuum in Edinburgh in the summer of 1992. They were held at the General Register House, the National Library of Scotland, the Royal Incorporation of Architects in Scotland's headquarters, and the National Monuments Record of Scotland. The publications here under review were the fruits of three of these exhibitions, but none is strictly a catalogue, and, consequently, they can be judged on their own merits.

The differing formats of the three works reflect their very different contents. Sanderson's, the largest, covers the whole of Adam's life; Brown's concentrates on one project, the publication of Diocletian's palace at Split in Croatia; the third approaches Adam's architecture from a multitude of angles in fifteen essays by thirteen contributors (including Brown and Sanderson).

In Margaret Sanderson's book which accompanied the exhibition at the Register House, one of Robert's few intact public buildings, we find a welcome biography, filling a gap left since John Fleming failed to supply the sequel to his classic *Robert Adam and his Circle* (1962), which dealt with the first half of his life and works. Sanderson fills out Fleming's picture with material more recently unearthed, and then continues the story up to his death. The buildings, though not ignored, act mainly as a backdrop to the family saga, centering around Robert, but not narrowly, so that we gain a portrait of a whole family. This makes for a very readable narrative in 134 pages, uninterrupted by detailed analyses of the works. It is difficult not to feel personally involved, as the story unfolds of the rise and fall of the brothers' fortunes, and of the estrangement of the eldest John, from the younger 'Adelphi'. One learns painlessly on the way much about mid-eighteenth century Edinburgh society, London Scots, the building trade, financial scandals, the personal and professional animosities which deprived us of the full-blooded South Bridge *Via Triumphalis* and of the Leith Street 'megastructure'. (I thank Ranald MacInnes for this term - see his article in this *Journal*). Sanderson demonstrates that there was a continuous Scottish thread to Adam's career even at the height of his success in London, and that the late flowering Scottish works were in ground already well-dug. The account is illustrated with a wealth of photographs of actual buildings, as well as engravings, and drawings and portraits of the principal characters.

In sum, it supplies an excellent introduction to the study of Adam's buildings.

Iain Brown's booklet concentrates on a single work of Adam's, the *Ruins of the Palace of the Emperor Diocletian at Spalatro in Dalmatia* (1764), explaining that the exhibition, which it accompanied, was suggested by Alistair Rowan to celebrate the National Library's recent acquisition of a set of annotated proof plates for *Spalatro*. In fifty-two generously illustrated pages Brown chronicles with economy and clarity the enormously complex undertaking of producing this *de luxe* contribution to archaeology. He begins by tracing how Adam settled on Diocletian's palace as the subject for his publication: not through any disinterested love of antiquity, but by cool calculation as to what would create the biggest impact on potential patrons with the least (he hoped) effort. Split merely fitted the bill as the nearest major unpublished collection of antiquities. While admiring his hard-headedness, I for one regret he dismissed his earlier scheme to publish Hadrian's Villa, Tivoli, and wonder if Adam felt similarly, given the difficulties of checking out measurements and details in the years after the initial five-week survey in 1757. At any time the difficulties of co-ordinating the production and correction of plates between Venice and London would have been formidable, without the complications of the Seven Years' War, and the quarrel with incorrigibly romantic and un-archaeologically minded Clerisseau, whose pivotal role is completely written out of the finished book. The irony is that by the time of its appearance, the original *raison d'être* was lost, since Adam's reputation was already established. All this is related in such a lucid manner by Brown as to be accessible to lay reader and scholar alike, while whetting appetites for his more detailed articles on aspects of Spalatro, which appeared during 1992.

The third publication, associated with the RIAS exhibition, is the most ambitious, collecting fifteen essays, grouped into four sections, the first, with pieces by Sanderson, Brown and David King, sets the scene with an overview of Robert's life and work. The second concentrates on particular aspects of his work: Gillian Haggart on classical villas, a particularly fruitful type for Adam in Scotland; Ranald MacInnes setting the public buildings within a European context; Jane Thomas on castles; Ben Tindall on Charlotte Square; Ian Gow, recognising William Adam's and continental influences on the interiors; and Bob Heath's intriguing suggestion that poor quality stone was deliberately quarried for the Culzean viaduct, to enhance its ruinous appearance. In the third part, Charles McKean and Mary Miers look at losses among Adam's oeuvre, while the fourth embraces survival with Jacky Chalmers discussing energy conservation in Charlotte Square, David King on Airthrey Castle and James Simpson on his restoration of 8 Queen St.

None of the essays is without interest, but the problem is that they are all crammed into fifty-six pages, liberally sprinkled with illustrations, with only Gow's and Miers's extending beyond two pages of text. While marvelling that the authors pack so much into so little, one wishes that those with larger themes could have been granted more space. Nevertheless, it is good that many of these questions have been raised, even if some go unanswered for the moment. Unfortunately the book is sold out and is no longer available.

Ian Campbell
Edinburgh College of Art/Heriot-Watt University

David King, *The Complete Works of Robert and James Adam*, Butterworth Architecture, Oxford, 1991. Published in association with the University of Stirling; hardback, £50.00, ISBN 07506 1286

As the statement on the dust-jacket puts it '[Mr King'] work has provided architectural literature with a unique and major reference source'. Mr King has, indeed, done an immense amount of work in tracking down references, matching drawings to buildings, and buildings to secondary sources, such as prints and photographs. There is a huge number of illustrations and a very welcome wealth of plans. The text, however, has problems, central to which is a certain metropolitan Anglo-centricity of approach, summed up, perhaps, by Mr King's classification of the 'early' work as beginning in 1760 when Robert Adam was in his thirty-second year.

'First-floor' principal storeys are described as 'curious' when in fact they are part of a Scots and European tradition. The Adams are corrected for referring to the ground floor of Hawkhill as such. It is 'really' Mr King explains 'a half-sunk basement'. As Ian Gow has said before, Scotland is mainstream European in this regard and, as a product of this culture, so is Adam.

The tradition established by Bolton, of attributing most of the later work in Scotland to James, is taken on board rather too uncritically. Doubt remains as to the authorship, for example, of the York Place church (it seems unlikely that the manse would have been an afterthought), and of the Tron Church proposals in Glasgow where the trustees had resolved to build anew in the 1780s, prior to the fire that destroyed the body of the existing church in 1793. Unfortunately, the whole issue remains unclear. Here, and in other secondary sources, much of the later work is described as being 'by the Adams' but at the Glasgow Infirmary, for example, we know that after the death of his brother, James was not at all keen to become involved, and had to be persuaded by his enterprising sister Betty to continue. In these circumstances, it is hard to imagine James taking on more work in Glasgow, but simply fulfilling existing contractual obligations. Perhaps, in the end, James Adam was a reluctant architect, more at home in the salon than on the building site. It may also be that the 'remote control' system effected by Robert from London with the assistance of John Paterson (and David Hamilton) in Scotland was by then so institutionalised as to allow quite complex projects to be carried out after Adam's death.

There is the familiar tenement problem, exemplified by Mr King's discussion of No. 1 Robert Street, Adelphi which he says was 'never occupied as a single dwelling'. An understanding of this building type leads to an explanation of what makes the Scottish town, from Inveraray to New Lanark, Glasgow, and Edinburgh, tend to monumentality of scale. And this tradition is central to an understanding of Adam, since it informs the planning of the megastructures of Bathwick, Leith Street, and the South Bridge. What would otherwise result in the 'prairie planning' of endless small houses is rendered monumental, in Scotland as in the rest of Europe through the tenement. Paterson had reported to Adam that the Town Council did not want the Charlotte Square dwellings 'set out in flates': Alexander Steven's answer, in executing the work, was, through an ingenious plan, to vary the tenement idea - basically the idea of sharing a roof structure - by placing vertically-divided dwellings in the pavilions where greater scale was required.

Like most authors, Mr King seems unwilling to situate Adam within the Scots architectural tradition. Edinburgh University, for example, is presented as if it were outside that tradition, bearing no historical relation to Glasgow University or to Scots public building, in spite of its double court and Holyrood entrance front. In the same way that David Hume is now seen as a 'product' of the Enlightenment in Scotland, we are beginning to see that Adam's work is unmistakably and thoroughly Scots: we have for too long taken far too literally his self-effacing statement that when he arrived in Italy he 'knew nothing'.

But Mr King should not, of course, be held personally responsible for any inferiorist malaise in Scottish architectural history. He is only the bearer of an ideology which we have been happy to go along with until quite recently. His work is an inventory rather than a re-assessment; he has been extremely tenacious in his research for which we should give him great credit, but he has had to rely on secondary material full of the familiar metropolitan attitudes and prejudices. No historian has yet attempted to place Robert Adam in a tradition which is neither pathologically old-fashioned nor simply some provincialised England.

Scots architecture, and its influence in Europe, North America and England, should be studied in its rightful context, without continual, often unnecessary, reference to England as the benchmark, and Mr King's book, with its most excellent photographic survey is an essential tool for that task.

Ranald MacInnes
Historic Scotland

Ian Gow, *The Scottish Interior*, Edinburgh University Press, 1992, hardback, £25.00,
ISBN 0 7486 0220 8

The inescapable fate of all but a tiny fraction of domestic interiors is that they will change appearance with extraordinary frequency. As a consequence they pose a tremendous challenge to the historian, who all too often has to resort to guess-work when attempting to recreate past arrangements. True, a great deal of information can be gleaned from inventories, but, even when these exist, they invariably fall short of conjuring up the reality of the lived-in home, telling us little, for example, about furniture arrangements or patterns and colours of wall hangings. Visual records, whether comprising paintings, engravings, drawings or photographs, are quite another matter and, supported by a sequence of informative and sharply observed essays, provide the basis for *The Scottish Interior*, in the shape of over two hundred images selected from the collections of the National Monuments Record of Scotland.

Selection has been based, in virtually every case, on historical reliability, an eminently sensible strategy that has been adhered to in the face of quite serious obstacles. The most immediately obvious of these is that it inevitably precludes all but a handful of pre-1800 interiors. Paintings and drawings executed before this date are, it seems, notoriously unreliable in terms of the provision of hard information, a criticism that is extended to a number of apparently carefully observed images of slightly later date, including Alexander Carse's The Arrival of the Country Cousins (1812), in which, we are informed, curtains have been removed and windows introduced in the interest of pictorial effect. For the same reason, (i.e. a limited stock of trustworthy sources) the interiors illustrated are almost all of the houses of the landed and well-to-do professional classes, sectors of society that have never accounted for more than a small proportion of the overall Scottish population.

The author's frustration at this state of affairs has determined the inclusion of a number of non NMRS sources, including Walter Giekie's c. 1820 study of the interior of a cottage in Cousland, Midlothian, one of a sequence of drawings contained in a sketch-book now in the possession of the National Gallery of Scotland. A significant aspect of this sketch is that it records a reasonably comfortable interior, arranged with impressive efficiency to accommodate cupboards, kists, box beds, a chair and a folding table, providing a useful antidote to the frequently pessimistic records of working class habitations left to us by so many later nineteenth century photographers who, responding to the traumas of industrialisation, invariably focused on the plight of the urban slum dweller, represented in this collection by a grandmother and child in an impoverished one-roomed dwelling.

With the perfection of photographic techniques in the late nineteenth and early twentieth century, the number of recorded interiors increased dramatically. Many of these images are of exceptionally high quality, and are not surprisingly assigned a prominent place in this anthology, which devotes, for example, a two page spread to the freshly complete Drawing Room of Hill House, Helensburgh, taken by the specialist architectural photographer Bedford Lemere. Others, produced by amateur photographers, are technically less competent but scarcely less interesting. Fourteen snapshots of 16 Leamington Terrace, Edinburgh are particularly remarkable in this respect, and afford the kind of insight into Edwardian middle class domesticity that social historians can normally only dream of attaining. At the very least, the information these contain should lead us to question the wisdom of too rigid an adherence to the notion of the period interior, evidenced in this case by what must surely have been an irregular accumulation of objects, brought together over an extended period to produce what the author describes as 'any layers of taste', and a Drawing Room that was neither 'smart' nor 'up-to-date'. Interestingly, something of the same quality is shown to have permeated the interiors of Sir Rowand Anderson's own house, 'Allermuir', the robust eclecticism of which will undoubtedly come as a surprise to many familiar with the building's exterior, which McKinstry has shown to have enjoyed an almost revolutionary significance, as the prototype for the distilled and simplified baronialism favoured by so many Scottish architects of the following generation.

This, then, is an unusually important book, that at last provides a Scottish counterpart to the already reasonably extensive literature devoted to the history of the English interior. Its publication seems certain to stimulate further research and will doubtless encourage a great many of us to look afresh at drawings and photographs in our own possession, some of which might conceivably be of interest to a successor volume which, the author informs us, is already being considered by the publishers, intended to focus on the period c. 1920 to the present.

John Frew
Department of Art History, University of St. Andrews.